classic
mexican
kitchen

classic
mexican
kitchen

Mexico's culinary heritage; ingredients, techniques, recipes

Jane Milton

southwater

This edition is published by Southwater

Southwater is an imprint of
Anness Publishing Limited
Hermes House
88-89 Blackfriars Road
London SE1 8HA
tel. 020 7401 2077
fax 020 7633 9499

Distributed in the UK by
The Manning Partnership
251-253 London Road East
Batheaston
Bath BA1 7RL
tel. 01225 852 727
fax 01225 852 852

Distributed in the USA by
Anness Publishing Inc.
27 West 20th Street
Suite 504
New York NY 10011
fax 212 807 6813

Distributed in Australia by
Sandstone Publishing
Unit 1, 360 Norton Street
Leichhardt
New South Wales 2040
tel. 02 9560 7888
fax 02 9560 7488

1 3 5 7 9 10 8 6 4 2

Publisher: Joanna Lorenz
Executive Editor: Linda Fraser
Senior Editor: Joanne Rippin
Project Editor: Helen Marsh
Consultant Editor: Jenni Fleetwood
Designer: Nigel Partridge
Photography: Simon Smith (recipes) and Janine Hosegood (reference)
Food for Photography: Caroline Barty (recipes) and Annabel Ford (reference)

The publishers would like to thank South American Pictures for the use of their photographs in the book:
8bl, tr; 9tl, br; 10t; 11tl, br; 12tl, tr, bl; 13tl, m, br; 14tr, ml, bl; 15tl, br; 16tr, bl;
17tl, br; 18tr, mr, bl; 19tr, ml, bl.

NOTES

For all recipes, quantities are given in both metric and imperial measures and, where appropriate, measures
are also given in standard cups and spoons. Follow one set, but not a mixture,
because they are not interchangeable.

Standard spoon and cup measures are level.

1 tsp = 5ml, 1 tbsp = 15ml, 1 cup = 250ml/8fl oz

Australian standard tablespoons are 20ml. Australian readers should use 3 tsp in
place of 1 tbsp for measuring small quantities of gelatine, cornflour, salt etc.

Medium eggs are used unless otherwise stated.

CONTENTS

INTRODUCTION

Mexican food mirrors the culture of the country — it is colourful, rich, stimulating and festive. From the wild and barren north to the sultry heat of the south, this vast country offers the food lover a feast of flavours. The waters of the Gulf of Mexico and the Pacific Ocean teem with fish, while the sub-tropical regions that adjoin them yield abundant fruit, including pineapples and papayas. From the gardens of the high plateau come wonderful vegetables, while the north is cattle country. Chillies of every shape, colour and size are everywhere, their flavours ranging from subtle to strident, providing the signature to one of the world's most exciting cuisines.

HISTORY OF COOKING IN MEXICO

Food is a very important aspect of the Mexican way of life. Producing and purchasing the raw materials, preparing food and eating it account for a large part of each day, and wonderful dishes are created to mark special occasions and celebrations.

Some Historical Influences on the Mexican Diet

In pre-Columbian Mexico there was already an established pattern of agriculture. Foods such as corn (maize), beans, chillies and peppers were widely cultivated, along with avocados, tomatoes, sweet potatoes, guavas and pineapples. Vegetables such as *jicama*, *chayote* and *sapote* were also grown.

During the Mayan era, the priests, who were the ruling class, allocated land for the growing of crops. They also arranged for the storage of seed and the distribution of surplus food. The warlike Aztecs, who came to power in the 15th century, were less inclined to share. Their rulers appropriated food for themselves, including chocolate, which was made into a frothy drink, believed to be an aphrodisiac.

The Aztecs inherited a rich culinary tradition. The central market in Tenochtitlan was famous for its fabulous array of foods and it is reported that Montezuma often required of his servants that they prepare more than two dozen dishes daily for his delectation. The emperor would then stroll among the groaning tables, discussing the ingredients with his chefs, before making his selection. During the subsequent meal, young women, chosen for their beauty, would bring him hot tortillas and gold cups filled with frothy chocolate.

Columbus Comes to Mexico

When the Spaniards first arrived in Mexico in 1492, they had few cooks with them, and so local people were hired to prepare food. Dishes made with corn, chillies, beans, tomatoes and chocolate were prepared and the Spaniards became particularly fond of chillies, chocolate and vanilla. With the Spanish came livestock, which was warmly welcomed. Until this time, the native turkeys and the occasional wild boar were the only source of meat.

The introduction of the domestic pig was significant not merely for its meat, but also for the lard, which was used for frying and became a staple ingredient in Mexican kitchens. Frying had not been possible before, due to the absence of

Below: A modern mural by Diego Rivera showing pre-Columbian corn sellers.

Above: Corn cultivation in Mexico's pre-Columbian era. Mural by Diego Rivera.

animal fats and oils. The Spaniards began to adapt their own recipes to the local ingredients, and the local people in turn adapted their cooking to include meat, which had been such a rarity in the past. The fusion began.

In 1519 the Spanish adventurer Hernando Cortés landed near the site of present day Veracruz. Within three years he had conquered Mexico, and the country was ruled as a viceroyalty of Spain for the next three hundred years. Cortés portrayed himself as the liberator of the tribes oppressed by the Aztecs and used his fanatical missionary zeal to justify his own exploitation of the Mexicans. Monks and nuns were sent from Spain to convert the pagan Mexicans to Catholicism. When they reached the New World, these religious missionaries had more than missals in their luggage; they also brought seeds, and soon citrus fruit, wheat, rice and onions augmented the supplies that served the Mexican kitchen.

Texas is Lost to the USA

Mexican independence from Spain was finally gained in 1821, after a lengthy war. Three years later, on the death of General Iturbide, a new republic was established. At that time Mexico possessed large tracts of land in what is

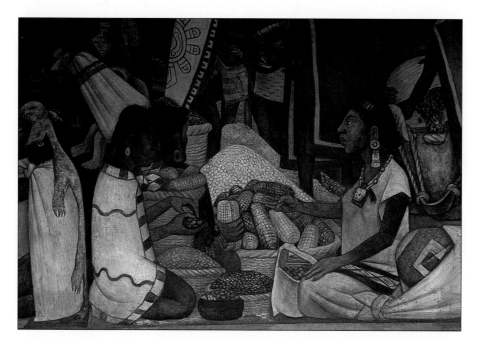

Above: Hernando Cortés, the Spanish conqueror of Mexico.

now the United States, including Texas. In 1836 Texas formed an independent republic, joining the USA some nine years later. This triggered the Mexican Civil War, as a result of which Mexico ceded to the United States all territories north of the Rio Grande. From a culinary perspective, this is significant, as it helps to explain the historic links between Mexico and the "Lone Star" State, and the origin of the Tex-Mex style of cooking. It also accounts for the popularity of the Mexican style of cooking in California and New Mexico.

French Occupation of Mexico

The Civil War proved costly in financial terms, and put the country greatly in debt to France, England and Spain. When they could no longer repay the debt to France, that country seized the opportunity to take control of Mexico. Austrian-born Maximilian Habsburg, a relative of Napoleon, was put in charge of the French occupation. The French met with considerable resistance and the *Cinco de Mayo* (5th May) holiday commemorates a famous Mexican victory over their forces. However, this success was short-lived, and France installed Maximilian as Emperor of Mexico in 1864. The French occupation lasted only three years, but left a lasting

legacy in the beautiful breads and pastries for which Mexican cooking is now renowned. Following Maximilian's execution in 1867, Mexico experienced another period of unrest, but since 1920 has been more stable.

Other Influences

The Mexican culture is often described as "*mestizo*". The word means "a mixture" and was originally applied only to the offspring of ethnic peoples and Spanish invaders. Today it reflects many culinary influences from beyond its borders, such as the introduction of brewing by German settlers. The Germans also introduced a cheese, now called *queso de Chihuahua* after the town in northern Mexico where the settlers lived. The presence of many sweet-and-sour

Below: Maya Indians in traditional dress perform the dance of the Mestizos.

dishes in the Mexican cuisine reflects an Oriental influence, as does the Mexican classification of foods as "hot" or "cold". This has nothing to do with the temperature at which these foods are served, but relates instead to the effect they have on the body. "Hot" foods are considered to be easily digested and warming, whereas foods designated as "cold" are held to be difficult to digest and likely to lower body heat. Examples of hot foods are coffee, honey and rice, while fish, limes and boiled eggs would all be regarded as cold. A proper balance between hot and cold foods is believed to be vital for good health.

Mexican cuisine is sure to continue to evolve, adapt and embrace foreign influences. It is also likely to become more homogenous as regional recipes are absorbed in the national repertoire. Like its language, the food and eating habits of a country are never static.

REGIONAL COOKING IN MEXICO

Mexico has not one single cuisine, but many. It is a vast country, the third largest in Latin America, with a wide diversity of landscapes, from snow-capped mountains to citrus groves, and a distinct range of climatic zones. These geographical factors have helped to shape a variety of different styles of cooking within the same country. The extremely mountainous nature of the landscape led in the days before the Spanish Conquest to the development of a large number of isolated and completely distinct Indian communities, each with its own style of cooking. When the Spanish invaded, they certainly had a considerable impact on the cuisine in the areas where they were most active, but parts of the country remained impervious to their influence, and the people there continued to cook in much the same

Above: Bananas and mangoes on sale in a street market in Chihuahua.

way as their parents and grandparents had done before them.

Even today, when tourism has introduced new ingredients and ideas, there remain pockets of Mexico where contact with the outside world is limited, and where old dishes, some of which hark back to Aztec times, are preserved.

The altitude, rather than the latitude, determines the climate in Mexico. The coastal region below 914m/3000ft is *tierra caliente* – the hot zone. Here the climate is sub-tropical, and mangoes, pineapples and avocados flourish. Next comes *tierra templada,* the temperate zone, which rises to 1800m/6000ft.

Culinary Regions
Even in present-day Mexico, regional foods are still very apparent. This is due in some measure to the different climates, which mean certain things cannot grow in every area, or to favourable geographic locations: in Vera Cruz, a coastal area, fish dishes are prevalent. In the coming years this is likely to be eroded more as improved transportation allows products from the different regions to be transported more easily and quickly between areas.

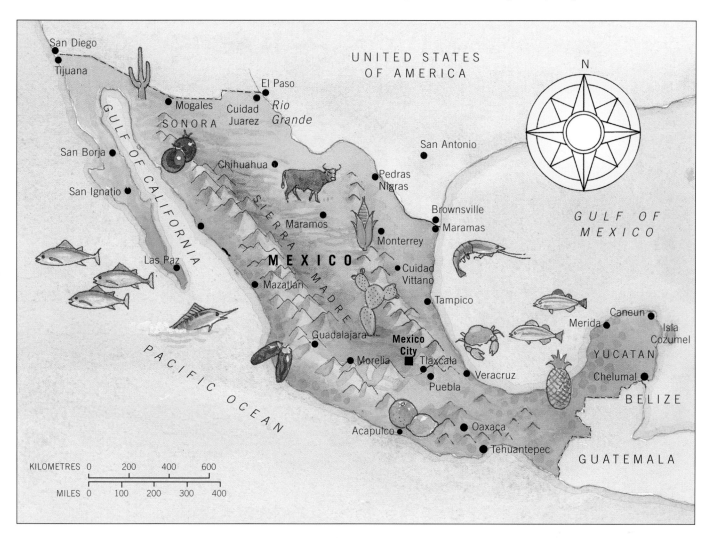

Above: Cooking tortillas in a Mexican street-cafe.

Many familiar vegetables and fruits are grown in Mexico, including green beans, peppers, tomatoes, cabbages, cauliflowers, onions, aubergines and courgettes. At the greatest altitude lies the cold zone (*tierra fria*).

These areas of Mexico are all very different from each other, and when it is considered that the rainfall varies from as little as 5cm/2in a year in the north-west to over 300cm/120in in parts of the south-west, it is easy to comprehend how so many diverse styles of cooking came to evolve. Better infrastructure may mean that the regionality of the cuisine will be eroded in time, but at the moment each region has a strong individual identity.

The North

The northern area of Mexico, stretching from Sonora, near the Gulf of California, to Monterrey in Nuevo León, has some striking contrasts. The mountain areas are sparsely populated and life here is very tough. Sonora and Chihuahua are the cattle rearing parts of Mexico. Good grazing encouraged the Spanish to establish herds of their hardy longhorns here, and specialities of the region

include a beef stew called *Caldiddo* and the famous dried beef or *carne seca*. This is produced by first salting the beef, then drying it and finally treating it with lemon juice and pepper.

The ubiquitous beans are as popular in the north as they are elsewhere. A favourite dish of the local *charros* or cowboys is *frijoles* (beans), cooked with scraps of meat, chillies, herbs and spices over an open fire. So well loved is the dish that it is often served in homes and restaurants.

Monterrey is the industrial heart of the region. Brewing employs a large percentage of the population, and this is the home of *frijoles borrachos,* a dish that consists of beans cooked in beer with onion, spices and garlic. The flavour of the beer permeates the beans, earning them their name, which translates as "drunken beans".

The north of Mexico is also the main cheese-producing region. Cheese was introduced by monks who travelled with the Spanish conquerors. Chihuahua is known for *chiles con queso* – melted cheese with chilli strips.The greatest treasure of the north is the soft flour tortilla, produced here because this is the only part of Mexico where wheat is grown. Burritos, portable parcels of meat, beans and rice wrapped in wheat flour tortillas, are typical of this region.

Baja California is a peninsula in the north-western corner of the country, bordering the Pacific and the Gulf of California. It is the oldest continuously producing wine-making region of Mexico. In recent years the region's wines, particularly the whites, have won international acclaim.

The Coastal Regions

The northern Pacific coast has some magnificent beaches. The sea is well stocked with fish, especially bass, tuna and swordfish. *Ceviche*, that delicious dish made of raw fish "cooked" by the action of lime juice, is very popular in the region. It is often made from prawns or other local shellfish.

This area generally has good soil, and grains of various types are widely cultivated, as well as chillies and other vegetables. So famous are the tomatoes produced in this region that the state basketball team is called *Tomateros* (the tomato growers). There are a number of coconut plantations along the coast, and dishes such as coconut soup are popular. Further south is the state of Jalisco, the home of tequila. Red snapper are caught on this part of the coast and cooked over open fires.

Below: Maguey, *growing here in the Oaxaca valley, is used in tequila.*

Above: Strings of chillies drying in the sun on the Pacific coast of Mexico.

Inland is the colonial town of Guadalajara, famous for *pozole*, a pork stew thickened with hominy – yellow or white corn which has been dried and has had the husk and germ removed, and which has been eaten by the Indians in Mexico for centuries. Another speciality is *birria*, a stew made from lamb or kid.

Down the coast is Acapulco, a very cosmopolitan city with Latin, Oriental and indigenous Indian influences. The cuisine of this area – Oaxaca – has strong Spanish influences, but is also home to some of the most traditional Mexican dishes, such as the *moles* – gloriously rich meat stews which incorporate nuts and chocolate. This is orange country, too, and citrus fruit features strongly in the recipes of the region. *Asadero*, a supple curd cheese similar to the Italian cheese, *Provolone*, originated in Oaxaca.

Chiapas, the southernmost state bordering Guatemala, exhibits some influences from that country. Chillies are commonly served alongside dishes, as accompaniments, rather than as integral ingredients.

The eastern seaboard, lapped by the Caribbean Sea, is known as the Gulf Coast. The climate here is tropical, and this is reflected in the food. Bananas, vanilla, avocados, coffee and coconuts grow on the coast, mangoes and pineapples in the south, and to the north are orchards of apples and pears.

The Gulf Coast has abundant fish stocks. The southern state of Tabasco, on the isthmus of Tehuantepec, is

Below: A palm tree in Chetumal with coconuts ready for harvesting.

Above: Prickly pear cactus growing at Santa Bulalia.

particularly famous for its fish. The catch includes sea bass, striped bass, crabs, lobsters and prawns. The port of Veracruz has a famous fish market, with red snapper the local speciality. The cuisine in this area is rich, and many of the towns have lent their names to dishes or ingredients.

In this part of Mexico, *tamales* (little filled parcels) are rolled in banana leaves, rather than the corn husks which are used elsewhere. Another local speciality is *jicama*, a crisp vegetable, which is served raw with a sprinkling of lime juice and ground chillies.

The Bajio, Central Mexico and Mexico City

To the north of Mexico City is the Bajio, a fertile area bordered by mountains. This is sometimes referred to as Colonial Mexico, and many of the local specialities are distinctly Spanish in origin, such as stuffed tongues and rich beef stews. Traditional Mexican foods are to be found here too, especially *nopales* (cactus paddles) and prickly pears (cactus fruit). *Pulque* – the drink made from the juice of the agave (or century) plant – is popular in this area. Pork is the favourite meat, often served as *Carnitas*. These are pieces of pork which are cooked in lard flavoured with orange, until the outside of each piece is crisp, while the inside is beautifully tender and succulent.

Central Mexico, a land-locked area, lies to the south of Mexico City, and includes the towns of Puebla and Tlaxcala. Puebla is the home of the classic dish, *Chiles en Nogada*, which

consists of stuffed chillies dipped in batter, then fried and served with a walnut sauce. Puebla is also associated with the famous *Mole Poblano*, which was said to have been invented by nuns in a local convent. *Mole Poblano* is a wonderfully complex dish in which turkey or chicken is cooked in a paste made by mixing crushed dried chillies, cinnamon and cloves, with sesame seeds and ground nuts, as well as onion, garlic and sometimes tomatillos.

Tlaxcala, which means "the place of many tortillas" is a town renowned for its food. Chicken stuffed with fruit and nuts is one popular dish, while another consists of lamb cooked in agave leaves. Both are usually washed down with the local *pulque*.

Vast, sprawling and vibrant, Mexico City is one of the most cosmopolitan places on earth, a fact that is reflected in its food. It is often said that Mexicans love to eat and would eat all day if they could, and in Mexico City there is nothing to stop them. The streets are filled with vendors selling all sorts of snacks. Some offer tortas and tortillas filled with various meats (including the chorizo for which nearby Toluca is famous), cheeses, beans and chillies. Others sell *tamales*, *sopes* and tacos to the commuters who rush past on their way to work. Another item available on

Above: Dried chillies and other fruit for sale on the streets of Mexico City.

Below: Thick tortillas are served here with cooked meats, chillies and beans.

market stalls is *cuitlacoche*, a corn fungus which tastes like a flavoursome mushroom. This has been regarded as a delicacy since pre-Columban times. *Cuitlacoche* is cooked and used to fill *crepas* (crepes), which the Mexicans adopted into their cuisine after the French occupation in the 19th century.

The South

Although there are differences between all the regions of Mexico, it is in the Yucatán that these are most marked. This is partly due to the isolation of the area, which was for centuries cut off from the rest of the country by dense jungle and swampland. The Maya lived here before the conquistadors came to Mexico, and their influence on the cooking can still be seen, particularly in *pibil*-style dishes, which got their name from the *pib* or pit in which they were steamed in Mayan times.

Although the poor soil does not readily support agriculture, corn is grown in areas where the vegetation has been cut and burned, and is ground to make meal, *masa harina*, which is used for corn tortillas and a host of other Mexican dishes. The pungent herb *epazote* is used in the cooking of this region, imparting a distinctive flavour.

Good fish, squid and shellfish, including the large prawns for which the area is well known, are available all along the coast. *Ceviche* is a popular dish, and is made from several different types of fish and shellfish, either singly or in combination.

Huevos Motuleños, a dish of eggs with refried beans and tomato sauce, is a well known Yucatec dish. Also typical of the area are dry spice pastes, called *recados*. These are mixtures of dried spices and vinegar or citrus juice, which are rubbed on to meat before it is cooked. *Recados* are made throughout the country, but they are particularly popular in the Yucatán. Some include ground achiote seed (annatto powder), which is valued for the earthy flavour and bright yellow colour it imparts. Another hallmark of Yucatec cooking is the habañero, a fiery chilli which is grown exclusively in the region.

Below: A field of corn on the cob drying on the plants.

MEXICAN MEAL PATTERNS

Many of the traditional Mexican dishes are very labour-intensive, reflecting the old society where the women worked all day long collecting the food required and then preparing it. Today, despite industrialization, the traditional meal patterns are still observed, especially in rural areas. Most Mexicans still eat their main meal in the middle of the day, and follow it by a siesta. Even in the cities, where meals are beginning to conform to the international pattern of breakfast, lunch and dinner, the biggest meal of the day is still eaten at lunchtime.

Desayuno

This is a light meal eaten first thing in the morning, soon after waking. It usually consists of a cup of coffee and a bread or pastry – perhaps *churros* or *pan dulce* (sweetened bread).

Almuerzo

Having started work very early in the morning, most Mexicans are ready for something fairly substantial by about 11am. Almuerzo is more brunch than

Above: Prickly chayote*, used in Mexican salads and vegetable dishes.*

Below: Green chillies for sale in a Mexican market.

Above: Women prepare the main family meal in a rural Mexican kitchen.

breakfast, and usually includes an egg dish such as *Huevos Rancheros* or scrambled eggs with salsa and cheese. Tortillas are served, and coffee, milk or fruit juice washes everything down.

Comida

This is the main meal of the day, generally eaten at a leisurely pace from about 3pm. The meal is made up of several courses. Soup is almost always served, and this is followed by a rice or pasta dish. The aptly named *platillo fuerte* – the phrase means "heavy dish" – is the main attraction. This dish is accompanied by tortillas, salad and pot beans or Refried Beans. The clay pot used to cook the pot beans – *Frijoles de Olla* – adds flavour to them. Garlic, coriander, onion and stock with chillies are additional ingredients, and cream or cheese is stirred in just before serving. The meal closes with *postre* (dessert) and an after-dinner coffee.

Merienda

A light supper, this is often made up from the leftovers of the lunchtime *comida* dishes, which are wrapped in a tortilla to make a burrito. If a more substantial meal is required, a stew or *mole* might be served, with *Cafe con Leche* or hot chocolate to follow the food. *Merienda* is usually eaten between 8 and 9pm.

Cena

This more elaborate meal – dinner – is served when entertaining guests in the evening or on special occasions. It replaces the *merienda* and is made up of two or three courses served any time between 8pm and midnight.

The Main Event

Comida – the main meal of the day – provides the perfect opportunity for relaxing with family or friends. Here are some suggestions of suitable dishes to serve at this time:

Sopa

A hearty soup would not be appropriate, as this is the prelude to a large meal. *Thalpeno*, a thin soup with chicken and avocado, would be ideal, as would a cold coconut soup.

Sopa Seca

Translating as "dry soup" this is actually a rice or pasta dish, served after the conventional soup and before the main course. Rice or vermicelli is cooked in a little oil and then simmered in a broth with onions, garlic, tomatoes and other vegetables. Most of the liquid used is absorbed by the rice or pasta, hence

the name. The rice dishes vary – peas are sometimes added to the basic recipe, and coriander and chillies are used to make the popular "Green Rice". In another variation, yellow rice is flavoured and coloured with achiote (annatto), a golden colouring made from the ground seeds of a flowering tree.

Pescado y Legumbres

Sometimes a fish course is served before the main dish. Typically this would be *Ceviche* – raw fish "cooked" by the action of lime juice. Alternatively, a vegetable dish might be offered; perhaps a native vegetable such as *jicama*, served as a salad with a chilli and lime dressing. Plantains are also popular, and either these or courgettes might be fried along with cheese and green chillies.

Platillo Fuerto

The "heavy dish" is typically a stew, served with corn tortillas and a salad. Meatballs in a tomato and chilli sauce is one option; pork with green cactus sauce another. A fisherman's stew of mussels, scallops, prawns and cod would also be suitable. For the accompaniment, a cactus or *chayote* salad would be ideal, or a fresh-tasting salsa of *rajas con limon* – strips of chilli and lime.

Above: A family eating their main meal in an open-air restaurant in Mexico City.

Frijoles

Cooked dried beans are an inevitable – and important – part of the main meal. Traditionally, they formed a very big part of the staple diet of the indigenous people, so the number and variety of bean dishes is exhaustive. Most people, if asked to name a Mexican bean dish, suggest Refried Beans, which is all too often a flavourless mush of badly seasoned pinto beans. The home-cooked equivalent couldn't be more different: tender beans deliciously flavoured with bay leaves, garlic and chillies. Equally delicious are pot beans, *Frijoles de Olla* – dry pinto beans put into a pot and cooked very slowly with water and a little lard until they melt in the mouth. These are traditionally served with Guacamole, salsa, soured cream and crumbled fresh cheese.

Postre y Cafe

After such a heavy meal, the dessert often consists of a fruit platter or a simple, refreshing *Flan* – similar to a crème caramel. A cake made from ground pecan nuts and honey is another favourite. *Comida* traditionally concludes with a drink of coarsely ground coffee sweetened with *piloncillo*

(the unrefined dark brown cane sugar typical of Mexico) and stirred with a cinnamon stick. A delicious alternative, which packs rather more punch, is coffee with a shot of Kahlúa or tequila.

Snack Foods

Mexicans love to snack. Street food is very popular throughout the country. In towns, stalls equipped with steamers sell *tamales* – little corn husk parcels filled with spiced meat or cheese – from first thing in the morning, so that shift workers can still have their *almuerzo* even if they cannot get home. Later in the day, the stalls sell corn soup or *menudo*, a soup made with tripe. Still more stalls are set up at lunchtime by women who serve home-made food to the workforce. The food is very similar to what would be eaten at home: soup, rice or pasta dishes, stews with tortillas or bread, and desserts. In the evening, the stalls sell *quesadillas*, enchiladas and *antojitos* (little whims or nibbles). On the coast, traders sell prawns on skewers, *Ceviche* (marinated raw fish) threaded on sticks or *elotes* – tender cobs of cooked corn dipped in cream and sprinkled generously with well-flavoured crumbly cheese.

Below: Corn on the cob is cooked and sold as a snack in street stalls.

FEASTS AND FESTIVALS

Long before Christianity came to Mexico, the Indians worshipped gods whom they believed provided their food. The Aztecs were convinced that the world would come to an end unless the gods were constantly propitiated with prayers, sacrifices and rituals. Corn (maize) was regarded as a divine gift – a miraculous staple food which grew in all climates and soils.

Feast days, when people cooked particular dishes or brought specific foods as offerings to the gods, were frequent events. When Christianity spread through Mexico many of these days were appropriated by the Church and either assigned as saints' days or linked to celebrations marking important days in the religious calendar.

January 6th – *Día de los Santos Reyes*

As the culmination of two weeks of Christmas festivities, January 6th marks the meeting between the Magi – the Three Kings – and the infant Jesus. Mexicans commemorate that exchange of gifts with ceremonies of their own, and this is the day on which Christmas presents are given and received. Central to the celebration is King's Day Bread, a yeasted sweet bread ring filled with crystallized fruit, covered with icing and decorated with candied fruit jewels.

Right: Maya Indians in traditional dress perform a bottle dance.

Below: A Mexican dancer wearing a Spanish-influenced traditional dress.

February – Carnival

The weekend before the beginning of Lent sees the beginning of a five-day carnival, a final fling before the period of self-denial. Processions of brightly coloured floats, dancing in the street and feasting are all characteristic of this celebration.

April – *Semana Santa*

Holy week – the period leading up to Easter Day – is an important time in the Mexican calendar, particularly for the many Catholics in the country. One custom peculiar to Mexico is the breaking of confetti-filled eggs over the heads of friends and family.

May 5th – *Cinco de Mayo*

This day commemorates the defeat of the French army at the Battle of Puebla in 1862. After the defeat Napoleon sent 30,000 soldiers into the country, and after a year the French had taken power. *Cinco de Mayo* is of particular importance in the state of Puebla, but is celebrated in other parts of the country and in some American states with large Mexican populations such as southern central California and Texas. Nowadays the holiday is a celebration of Mexican culture, drink and music.

Above: Sugar skulls on sale for the celebration of one of Mexico's most important festivals, The Day of the Dead.

September 16th – Mexican Independence Day

A holiday to mark the day in 1810 when the revolt against Spanish rule began. Outside Mexico, the festival is often promoted by commercial outlets, such as Mexican restaurants and bars.

November 1 & 2 – *Los Días de los Muertes*

Commonly called The Day of the Dead, this is in fact a two-day festival, that combines in one both the ancient Aztec tradition of worship of the dead and the Christian festival of All Saints' Day.

The festival originally came about because of a widely held belief that the souls of the dead are permitted to spend a brief period on earth every year – like a holiday – to give their families a chance to spend time with them. Family members gather at the graveside, bringing the favourite foods of the deceased person, as well as other symbolic dishes that are traditionally eaten on this day. The foods include a sweet pumpkin dessert and *tamales*. At the grave candles are lit, incense is burned, special prayers are said and the food and drink are eaten in a party atmosphere. Although the festival commemorates the dead, it is seen by everyone as a joyous occasion. The Mexican attitude is that life is to be lived to the full, and death is simply a part of the cycle.

December 25th – *Navidad*/Christmas Day

For 12 days before Christmas Day, the festival is heralded by processions – called "*posadas*" – depicting Joseph, with Mary on the donkey, searching for a room at the inn. Christmas Day sees

Below: A shop window advertises "bread of the dead" for the festival.

the start of a two-week family holiday for most Mexicans. On the afternoon of the day itself families share a special meal. This traditionally starts with the sharing of the *rosca* – a sweet ring-shaped loaf with a small ceramic doll representing the infant Jesus baked inside it. Whoever finds the doll in their slice of cake must host a party on February 2nd, *Día de Candelaria* (Candlemas). The high point of the Christmas feast is the main course, when *Mole Poblano*, a rich turkey dish made with chillies, nuts, tomatoes, garlic, cinnamon and chocolate is served. It is accompanied by *tamales blancos* – corn husk parcels filled with a flavoured mixture that is based on white cornmeal.

Mexican Weddings

These almost always take place in church. It is traditional for the bride and groom to be united during the ceremony with a *lazo* – a large rosary which is wrapped around them both. Gold or silver coins, a Bible and a rosary are given to the couple during the service by the "*padrinos*", a man and woman especially chosen by the bride and groom for this task. The coins symbolize prosperity. Mexican wedding cookies are served at the subsequent feast. Made from almonds and butter, baked and then sprinkled with icing sugar, these have a shortbread-like texture.

MEXICAN COOKING OUTSIDE MEXICO

Over the past decade in the UK and for a longer period in the USA there has been a tremendous growth in the number of Mexican restaurants and establishments serving what has come to be known as Tex-Mex food – Mexican food with a Texan influence. Sadly, these restaurants are not always very representative of the wonderful and varied cuisine Mexico has to offer, but what they have done is to stimulate interest in Mexican food and therefore a demand for more authentic Mexican ingredients and equipment. The growing popularity of Mexico amongst tourists has created even more of an interest in the country's varied cuisine.

USA

Mexicans who have emigrated to the United States for political, economic or personal reasons have created their own communities within that country. Parts of the United States such as southern California and Texas, which have strong historical links to Mexico as well as sharing a common border, have large communities of Mexicans and offer some of the best Mexican food. The Mexican cuisine in these areas has

Below: Mexican chillies, when dried, are exported all over the world.

Above and below: Fast-food stalls serving Mexican or Tex-Mex food are a common sight all over America, especially in the South. These two stalls are in New Mexico.

evolved over time to please the palates of local residents. Authentic Mexican ingredients are used, but American products are as well. This style of cooking is often referred to as "fusion", the mixing together of ingredients and flavours from several cultures in one dish, a practice that carries with it the real danger of diluting each country's contribution and distorting the diners' perceptions of each cuisine. In southern California and Texas, however, authentic Mexican ingredients tend to be readily available, thanks to demand and to the proximity to the border, and improved transportation links across Mexico and into the United States ensure that products arrive fresh and undamaged.

The same cannot be said for the rest of the United States. Availability of authentic Mexican ingredients varies from state to state, and some fruits and types of chilli are difficult, if not quite impossible, to obtain.

Other items, such as pinto beans, squash, avocados and chocolate, have become such an integral part of the American diet that few people would consider them to be Mexican foods.

Europe

With the growing number of European people taking holidays in Mexico, the trend for new culinary flavours or

experiences and the increasing market for travel features on television and in magazines, interest in Mexican cuisine has escalated. Nowhere is this more apparent than in Scandinavia, where Mexican food is enormously popular.

Increased demand has led to more varieties of fresh and dried chillies becoming available in both major supermarkets and specialist stores, and this in turn has persuaded more people to experiment with cooking Mexican food at home. The most significant advance in recent years has been the introduction of ready-made corn and flour tortillas in supermarkets and in heat-sealed packs which can be kept in the store cupboard until needed, when they are heated very briefly in the microwave. These have made many dishes much more accessible to the average home cook. People for whom Mexican food meant serving chilli in a taco shell – and who were put off by the sheer messiness of this awkward dish –

Above: Tequila husks. Tequila has grown in popularity around the world.

Below: An American fast-food stall selling Mexican-inspired roasted corn.

discovered ready-made tortillas and were soon experimenting with making fajitas and enchiladas, at first using prepared sauces and ready meals, but then becoming more adventurous. Supermarkets sell ready-made Guacamole, but in order to give this the required shelf life, add extra ingredients such as mayonnaise which dull the fresh, clean taste of the original dish. More discerning cooks prefer still to make their own.

Burritos, nachos and chimichangas are becoming well known, with cooks beginning now to differentiate between Mexico's regional cuisines. Just as the more regional Indian restaurants have persuaded the public that the whole of India cannot be represented by "chicken curry", so people are becoming familiar with the variety and depth of Mexican cuisine and are beginning to seek out more authentic Mexican dishes.

Good quality, reasonably priced Mexican ingredients are available by mail order from a number of specialist suppliers, and this has made it much easier for the enthusiast to recreate genuine dishes at home. Traditional Mexican cooking equipment such as *metates* (used for grinding *masa harina*) and the *molcajete* and *tejolote* (the

Above: Chocolate is now so widespread that people don't necessarily link it with its country of origin, Mexico.

Mexican pestle and mortar) are also available through mail order, but many of the functions for which these utensils are intended are either not necessary or can be carried out just as quickly and efficiently in a food processor.

Restaurants

In America and to a lesser extent in Europe, a number of restaurant chains specializing in Mexican and Tex-Mex food have been established. Tex-Mex restaurants tend to offer burgers and steaks alongside predominantly tortilla-based dishes, so it is not surprising that many people perceive these as being all that Mexico has to offer. Even some restaurants purporting to serve authentic Mexican food perpetuate the myth that Mexicans eat plates piled high with indistinguishable mounds of food, all fairly bland, covered with melted cheese, dollops of soured cream, Guacamole and salsa. In the United States there is an increasing number of small restaurants serving authentic dishes from all over Mexico. A welcome trend indeed.

EQUIPMENT

You need very little by way of specialist equipment in order to cook Mexican food. Most modern Mexican kitchens today have a food processor to do much of the chopping and grinding. However, the items listed below will make many of the tasks easier and are worth investing in if you make a lot of Mexican food.

Tortilla Press

Traditionally, tortillas were always shaped by hand. Skilled women were able to make an astonishing number of perfectly shaped tortillas in a very short time, but this is something of a dying art today. Most people now use metal tortilla presses. Cast iron presses are the most effective, but they must be seasoned (oiled) before use and carefully cared for, so many people today prefer steel presses. These come in various sizes and are heavy, in order to limit the leverage required to work them. Cover the plates with plastic bags or waxed paper and it will be easier to lift the tortillas once they are pressed. Tortilla presses are available in good specialist kitchenware shops and by mail order.

Comal

This is a thin, circular griddle, traditionally used over an open fire to cook tortillas. A cast iron griddle or large frying pan will do this job equally well.

Right: Tortilla press

Above: Metate

Below: Comal

Metate

A *metate* is a grinding stone used to grind corn to make *masa*. It is also used to grind cocoa and *piloncillo* (unrefined cane sugar). The design has not changed for centuries. Made from a sloping piece of volcanic rock, it has three short legs. Before a new *metate* can be used, it must be tempered. A mixture of dry rice and salt is placed on the grinding surface and the *muller* – the implement that does the actual grinding – is used to press the mixture into the surface and remove any loose pieces of sand or grit. The *muller* is made of the same stone as the *metate* and is called a *mano* or *metlapil*. These are quite difficult to locate outside Mexico, but are available by mail order.

Molcajete and Tejolote

The mortar and pestle of Mexico, the *molcajete* and *tejolote* are made from porous volcanic rock and must be tempered in the same way as the *metate* before being used. They are ideal for grinding spices such as achiote (annatto) or for grinding nuts and seeds when making *Mole Poblano*.

Tortilla Warmer

Ideal for keeping tortillas warm at the table, this is a small round basket or clay dish with a lid. The size most readily available outside Mexico is suitable for 15cm/6in tortillas. Look for them in specialist kitchenware shops.

Below: Molinollo *and wire whisk*

Right: Molcajete *and* Tejolote

Left: Dishes

Ollas

These are the clay pots traditionally used for cooking stews and sauces. They give food a unique flavour, but are seldom to be found outside Mexico, as they are quite fragile. Sadly, they are becoming relatively rare in Mexico too. Flat earthenware dishes decorated around the edge are used for serving and are more easily found than *ollas*.

Molinollo

A carved wooden implement used for whisking drinking chocolate. Some of these are beautiful and are popular with tourists. A wire whisk can also be used.

Above: Ollas

INGREDIENTS

Across the length and breadth of Mexico, the very different types of terrain and variations in climate provide a remarkable range of ingredients. Mexicans are very resourceful, and have made good use of their native foods, as well as adapting many of the ingredients and recipes brought by successive settlers. Some of their favourite foodstuffs will be familiar; others will be unusual; still more may seldom be seen outside their country of origin, but as the popularity of Mexican food continues to soar, demand increases and ingredients that were once rare become commonplace. This chapter is a guide to key ingredients, and offers advice on purchasing, preparing and storing, as well as cooking tips.

CORN (MAIZE AND FLOUR)

The native Indians of Mexico regarded corn as a gift from the gods. How else would they have come by such a versatile food, so hardy and adaptable and able to flourish in all the different climates and soils of their country? They offered up gifts to the god of corn, celebrated him on feast days and even added tiny grains of corn pollen to their traditional sand paintings to give the artworks healing powers. A popular myth held that corn was in fact the very stuff from which the gods created people. Even now, corn accounts for almost 20 per cent of the world's calories taken from food.

In the traditional Navajo Indian wedding ceremony, the bride's

Above: White corn

grandmother presents the couple with a basket of cornmeal and the couple exchange a small handful with each other – such is the significance of corn in their culture.

Every part of the corn cob is used in Mexican culture: the husks for wrapping *tamales*, the silk in medicines, the kernels for food and the stalks for animal feed. The husks from corn cobs are most commonly used for *tamales*, but are also used for wrapping some other foods before cooking. When they are ready, the husks will peel away from the filling. The husks are not eaten, but are discarded once the *tamales* are cooked. In Oaxaca *tamales* are wrapped in banana leaves, which impart a distinctively different flavour.

Varieties and Uses

Corn is the common name for a cereal grass. With wheat and rice, it is one of the world's key grain crops. A native of the Americas, it was introduced into Europe by Columbus, who brought it to Spain. A wide variety of products are produced from corn, including corn syrup, bourbon and starch.

Hybrid varieties of corn can be produced very easily as corn mutates

and adapts to different surroundings readily. There are a few main types of corn used for food, each with several different varieties.

Flint corn This is also known as Indian corn and is described as "flint" because of the hard texture of the kernel. This can be red, blue, brown or purple, which has made this type of corn a popular choice for some of the more novel foods such as blue or red corn tortilla chips. Popcorn is made from a type of flint corn. Predominantly, however, flint corn is used for industrial purposes and animal feed.

Yellow corn A type of "dent" corn, so called because the sides of the kernel are composed of a hard starch and the crown of a softer starch which shrinks to form the characteristic depression or dent. Yellow corn has large, full-flavoured kernels and is used for making many processed foods. It is also the basic ingredient used in corn syrup, cornstarch and corn oil.

White corn is used to make *masa*, a type of dough that is widely used in Mexican cooking. It may seem odd to call it white corn, when the resulting *masa* is actually quite yellow, but the kernels are noticeably whiter than those of yellow corn varieties.

Flour corn is composed largely of soft starch and can readily be ground to make flour for use in baked products.

Above: Blue corn

Below: Corn husks; fresh and dried

Below: Red corn

Preparing Dried Corn Husks

If you are able to buy dried corn husks you will need to make them soft and pliable before using.

Soak the corn husks in a bowl of cold water for several hours. When they are soft, remove them from the bowl and pat dry.

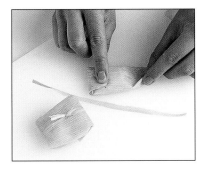

Place the husks flat on a dry surface. Pile on the filling, then tie in neat parcels before steaming.

Grinding produces the very white cornflour with which we are familiar, and which is the main constituent of custard powder.

Sweetcorn contains more natural sugar than other types of corn. The kernels can be eaten straight from the cooked cob and in Mexico a favourite snack is *elotes con crema*, where the corn cobs are dipped in cream and sprinkled with fresh cheese before being served. The kernels can also be stripped from the cobs and used in soups and vegetable dishes. As soon as the cob is picked, the sugar in the kernels starts to convert to starch. This reduces the natural sweetness, so it is important that the corn is eaten as soon as possible after being picked. Strip off the husks and remove the silks (the thread-like stigmas that catch the pollen) before boiling or steaming the cobs, or baking them in the oven. Sweetcorn can also be cooked on a grill or barbecue, which gives the crisp kernels a delicious smoky taste. This is how the Mexicans cook sweetcorn on the street as a fast food snack.

Masa/Masa Harina

Masa is the Mexican word for dough, and specifically refers to the fresh corn dough used to make corn tortillas and other corn dishes. The flour – or *masa harina* is traditionally made with sun-dried or fire-dried white corn kernels which have been cooked in water mixed with lime (calcium oxide, not the fruit). They are then soaked in the lime water overnight. The lime helps to swell the kernels and brings about a chemical change which greatly improves the flavour of the *masa*. The wet corn is subsequently ground, using a *metate* – a traditional grinding stone which no self-respecting Mexican kitchen would be without. The resulting *masa* can be used for making corn tortillas – for *tamales*, other ingredients, such as chicken stock and lard need to be added.

In America it is possible to buy fresh *masa* from the factories producing tortillas, but it is not available elsewhere. You can make your own *masa*, but it is a lengthy process and the essential lime is not easy to come by. If you do decide to have a go, it is well worth making a large batch of it and freezing the surplus. *Masa* freezes well, although it will only keep in the fridge for a few days.

Right: Two types of Masa harina

Above: Wet corn being ground on the traditional metate.

In some parts of Mexico they serve blue corn *masa* dishes, using the same dough-making process, but a less common corn type.

Corn Tortillas

Have ready a tortilla press and two clean plastic bags, slit if necessary so that they will lie flat. Tortillas are more traditionally cooked on a special griddle called a *comal*, but a cast-iron griddle or large heavy-based frying pan will work just as well.

MAKES 12 × 15CM/6IN TORTILLAS

INGREDIENTS
  275g/10oz/2 cups *masa harina*
  pinch of salt
  250ml/8fl oz/1 cup warm water

1 Place the *masa harina*, salt and water in a large bowl and mix together using a wooden spoon until it forms a dough.

2 Turn out the dough on to a lightly floured surface and knead well for 3–4 minutes until firm, smooth and no longer sticky. Cover the bowl with clear film and leave the dough to stand at room temperature for 1 hour.

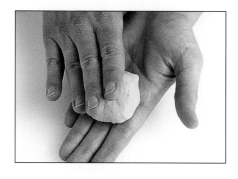

3 Pinch off 12 pieces of dough of equal size and roll each piece into a ball. Work with one piece of dough at a time, keeping the rest of the pieces of dough covered with clear film so that they do not dry out.

4 Open the tortilla press and place a plastic bag on the base. Put a dough ball on top and press with the palm of your hand to flatten slightly.

5 Lay a second plastic bag on top of the round of dough and close the press. Press down firmly several times to flatten the dough into a thin round.

6 Place a large frying pan or griddle over a moderate heat. Open the press and lift out the tortilla, keeping it sandwiched between the plastic bags. Carefully peel off the first bag, then gently turn the tortilla over on to the palm of your hand. Carefully peel off the second plastic bag.

7 Flip the tortilla on to the hot frying pan or griddle and cook for about 1 minute or until the lower surface is blistered and is just beginning to turn golden brown. Turn over using a palette knife and keep warm until ready to serve.

8 Place a clean dish towel in a large ovenproof dish. Transfer the cooked tortilla to the dish, wrap the dish towel over the top and cover with a lid. Keep warm while you cook the remaining tortillas in the same way.

COOK'S TIP
If you do not have a tortilla press, you can improvise by placing the dough between two clean plastic bags and rolling it out with a rolling pin.

Basic *Masa*
Traditionally, tortillas are made with *masa*. *Masa* is made by mixing dried white corn with food grade calcium oxide, although this is difficult to locate in small quantities. For making tortillas, most cooks, even in Mexico, find it easier to use *masa harina*, which is the flour made when *masa* is dried and ground. *Masa harina* should not be confused with cornmeal, polenta or maize meal, all of which are made from corn, but without being soaked or cooked with lime. The taste of tortillas made with *masa harina* is slightly different from that of tortillas made from fresh *masa*, but the flour is much easier to cook with and does away with the need for a *metate*.

Flour Tortillas

Wheat flour tortillas are more common than corn tortillas in the north of Mexico, especially in the areas around Sonora and Chihuahua, where wheat is grown. Flour tortillas differ from corn tortillas in that they include lard, which gives them more pliability and elasticity. For best results, make sure you use a good quality plain flour.

MAKES ABOUT 12 × 25CM/10IN TORTILLAS

INGREDIENTS

 500g/1¼ lb/5 cups plain flour, sifted
 2.5ml/½ tsp baking powder
 pinch of salt
 100g/3¾ oz/scant ½ cup lard
 about 120ml/4fl oz/½ cup
  warm water

1 Mix the flour, baking powder and salt in a large bowl. Rub in the lard, then gradually add enough water to draw the flour together into a stiff dough.

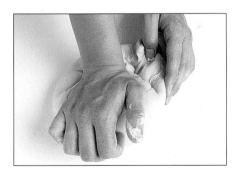

2 Turn out the dough on to a lightly floured work surface and knead it for 10–15 minutes until it is elastic.

3 Divide the dough into 12 even-size pieces and roll into balls using the palms of your hand. Cover the pieces with clear film while you are working to stop them drying out.

4 Roll out each ball on a lightly floured surface. Give the dough a quarter turn after each roll to keep the round even. Keep rolling until the round is about 30cm/12in.

5 Warm a large heavy-based frying pan or griddle over a medium heat. Cook one tortilla at a time, placing each one in the ungreased pan or on the griddle and cooking it for 45 seconds–1 minute or until the lower surface begins to blister and brown. Turn over and cook the other side for about 1 minute.

6 Wrap the cooked tortillas in a clean, dry dish towel to keep them soft and warm while you make the rest.

COOK'S TIPS

• If the corn tortillas crack when they are pressed, remove the dough from the press, return it to the bowl and add a little extra water.
• To reheat cold tortillas, sprinkle them with a few drops of water, wrap them in foil and place in an oven preheated to 140°C/275°F/Gas 1 for 10 minutes. Alternatively, wrap them in clear film and microwave on maximum power for about 20 seconds.

Quick and Easy Tortilla Fillings

• Cut a skinned chicken breast into thin slices and stir fry with slices of red and yellow pepper. When the chicken is cooked add the juice of a lime and some fresh oregano, add salt and pepper to taste then use the mixture to fill freshly warmed tortillas. Add some grated cheese if you wish and a spoonful of sour cream.
• If you have some rice and refried beans left from the previous day, mix them together and reheat in a frying pan with a little oil. When the mixture is thoroughly heated spoon into the tortillas with some grated cheese, slices of tomato and chopped spring onions.
• Stir fry some mushrooms with plenty of black pepper. Add a dash of soy sauce and a little double cream, season to taste then spoon into the tortillas.

FOLDING AND COOKING TORTILLAS

Many Mexican dishes are made with tortillas. The difference lies in the filling, folding and cooking.

Burritos

These are flour tortilla envelopes enclosing various fillings and then folded into the classic shape and the edges sealed with flour and water.

Chimichangas

A chimichanga is a burrito that has been folded, chilled to allow the edges to seal and then deep fried in hot oil until crisp and golden.

Chalupas

Chalupas are pieces of *masa* shaped to resemble canoes or boats and fried until opaque and golden. They are topped with beans, salsa and cheese.

Enchiladas

These can be made from either corn or wheat tortillas. A little filling is laid down the centre of a tortilla, which is then rolled to make a tube, rather like cannelloni. Filled tortillas are laid side by side in a baking dish before being topped with a sauce and baked in the oven or finished under the grill.

Fajitas

These are ideal for informal dinner parties, as various fillings are placed on the table with the hot tortillas, and guests fill and roll their own. The tortilla is then folded to form a pocket around the filling.

Flautas

Corn tortillas are filled with a pork or chicken mixture, rolled tightly into flute shapes, then fried until crisp.

Quesadillas

These tasty treats are made by placing a corn or flour tortilla in a warm frying pan and spreading one half lightly with salsa. A little chicken or a few prawns are sometimes added, and fresh cheese is sprinkled on top. The other half of the tortilla is then folded over, and the quesadilla is cooked for 1–2 minutes, during which time it is turned once.

Tacos

The crisp tortilla shells which are often sold in supermarkets as tacos are in fact a Tex-Mex invention. True Mexican tacos are corn tortillas that have been filled and folded in half; they still remain soft. *Taquitos* are miniature tacos – ideal for picnics or parties.

Tostadas

These are individual corn tortillas fried until crisp and then topped with shredded meat, Refried Beans, salsa, Guacamole, soured cream and a little fresh cheese. The finger-food versions are called *tostaditas*.

Totopos

Triangles of corn tortilla, fried until crisp, are called *totopos*. Serve them with a salsa – they are delicious served while still warm.

READY-MADE TORTILLAS

Making Mexican meals is much easier than it once was, thanks to the availability of ready-made tortillas and tortilla chips.

Corn Tortillas

Many supermarkets stock 15cm/6in fresh corn tortillas. Look for them in the bread section. They are ideal for making tacos, tostadas, *totopos* and enchiladas. They do not have a very long shelf life but they do freeze well. Follow the manufacturer's instructions for warming them as methods vary.

Flour Tortillas

These are available in 15cm/6in, 20cm/8in and 25cm/10in sizes, and the packaging is usually marked in inches rather than centimetres. The smallest ones are perfect for fajitas or flour tortilla quesadillas, while the 20cm/8in tortillas are a good size for large quesadillas (to share). Use the largest tortillas for burritos and chimichangas as they allow more room for the filling. Like corn tortillas, fresh flour tortillas are sold in the bread section of supermarkets or in vacuum packs beside the ethnic food ingredients. The longer-life products tend to be a bit drier and less pliable than the fresh variety, which can be frozen. Flour tortillas sold in shops often contain lard, which makes them softer than the ones that use vegetable oil or fat.

Taco Shells

A Tex-Mex invention, these are so awkward to eat that they are responsible for putting many people off eating Mexican food. They are, however, an excellent substitute for *chalupas*, if making your own seems too much like hard work. Fill them with salsa, beans and fresh, crumbly cheese.

Tortilla Chips

The quality and authenticity of these vary greatly. The best are often to be found in the ethnic food sections of supermarkets rather than with the crisps and snacks. Many of the ones sold in the snack food section have added flavourings, some of which are not remotely Mexican. Plain, lightly salted chips are best for dipping with salsa. Many specialist food stores and health food stores sell organic corn chips and naturally coloured red and blue corn chips (made from coloured corn kernels). These look especially good mixed with yellow corn chips in a dish. Warm them in a low oven or microwave before serving.

Above: Corn tortillas

Below: Wheat flour tortillas

Above: Blue and yellow tortilla chips. Plain, lightly salted chips are best for dipping with salsa.

Below: Taco shells are difficult to eat but do have their uses.

BEANS AND RICE

The importance of beans in the Mexican diet cannot really be overestimated. Indigenous to the country, they were cultivated by the Indians along with corn, and the two staple crops coexisted in a remarkable fashion. Successive plantings of corn soon deplete the soil; beans enrich it by introducing nitrogen. The early inhabitants of Mexico sensed this, and planted both together. They ate them together too, and benefited from the fact that beans supplied nutrients corn lacked, and, unlike corn, were also an excellent source of protein. Rice was first introduced to Mexico by the Spanish and is also an important staple ingredient.

BEANS

Beans continue to be a staple food in Mexico, and there will be a pot of dried beans simmering daily on the cooker top in every home. Fresh beans are eaten, too, of course, but it is the dried beans, with their better keeping properties, that are most widely used. They make a colourful display on market stalls, and there are many different varieties to choose from.

Popular Varieties

Pinto beans and black beans are the most commonly used dried beans in Mexico, although lima beans, which are sold both fresh and dried, are used in a number of dishes and side dishes.

Chick-peas, which in Mexico are called garbanzos, are not native to the country, but were brought in from the Middle East. They have become popular, however, and feature in several dishes.

Pinto beans Pinto is Spanish for "painted" and refers to the speckles of red-brown on the pale pink skins. These beans are native to Latin America and are now widely used in most Spanish-speaking countries. A rich source of protein and iron, they are only available dried. Mexicans use them for all sorts of dishes, but it is as *Frijoles de Olla*, the simple bean dish that is eaten daily in most homes, that they are most familiar. The cooked beans are also the basis of *Refritos* (Refried Beans), and are used in salsas.

Black beans Small, with black skins and cream-coloured flesh, these beans have a wonderfully sweet flavour. Do not confuse them with black-eyed beans, which are white, with a small black eye. The glossy skins look particularly attractive after cooking. They are used in soups and salsas, and are often substituted for pinto beans in *Frijoles de Olla*. Despite their small size, black beans can take quite a long time to

Above: Pinto beans

soften when cooked, so always test before draining, to ensure that they are perfectly tender.

Buying and Storing

Dried beans keep very well, but not indefinitely, so it is best to buy them in relatively small quantities, from a shop with a rapid turnover. That way, they are likely to be tender and full of flavour when soaked and cooked, unlike beans that have been kept for too long, which become dry and so hard that they are only fit for use as weights in pastry cases. Store beans in tightly closed containers in a cool, dry place.

Preparation

Before you use dried beans, put them in a colander or sieve and pick them over, removing any foreign bodies, then rinse them thoroughly under cold running water. Drain, tip into a large bowl and pour over plenty of cold water.

Above: Black beans

Leave to soak for several hours, and preferably overnight. Alternatively, you can boil the beans in plenty of water for 3–4 minutes, then cover the pan and set it aside for an hour before cooking. This is very useful when you have forgotten to soak beans for a particular dish, although the long cold soak is preferable.

Main Uses and Cooking Tips

In Mexico, beans are widely used in soups, as fillings for tortillas, in many meat dishes and on their own, either freshly cooked or refried.

To cook pre-soaked dried beans, simply drain them thoroughly, then put them in a clean pan with plenty of water. Do not add salt, as this would cause the skins on the beans to toughen. Bring the water to the boil and then cook for the time recommended in the individual recipes, usually 1–1¼ hours.

Right: Long grain (top) and ground rice

Cooking times can vary considerably, so always taste for tenderness before finally draining and serving the beans.

RICE

Mexicans have been using rice since it was introduced to the country by the Spanish in the 16th century. It was originally brought to Mexico from the Philippines and was also shipped on to Spain itself.

Description and Varieties

The rice grown and used in Mexico is long grain – this means

that each grain is four times longer than its width. White long grain rice that has had the husk removed is most common, although it is often not as refined as the white rice most widely sold in the West.

Buying and Storing

Most rice for sale in the West comes in packets. It keeps extremely well in a cool, dry place, but once packets are opened, any unused rice should be transferred to an airtight container and used as soon as possible. For Mexican food, it is important to use a rice that absorbs the flavours of other ingredients well. It is usual to use ordinary long grain rice, but you may like to experiment with other types.

Main Uses and Cooking Tips

Rice is used in a variety of Mexican dishes, from *sopa seca* (dry soup), which is served as a separate course in the *comida* or main meal, to rice pudding. When served as an accompaniment, rice is usually mixed with other ingredients, as in the popular Green Rice, which includes chillies, and Yellow Rice, which owes its colour to achiote (annatto). Ground rice is used as a flour (*harina de arroz*) in cakes or biscuits. *Horchata* is a drink made with rice that has been soaked and then finely ground. Most Mexicans tend to soak their rice in boiled water for a minimum of 10 minutes before they cook it. This reduces the cooking time and also encourages the rice to absorb other flavours. After soaking, it should be drained thoroughly before being cooked.

CHOCOLATE, NUTS AND SEEDS

Sweets, puddings, cakes and pastries are much loved by the Mexicans, but the sweet ingredients that go into these are also used in savoury dishes, and chocolate, along with various types of nuts and seeds are very important elements of Mexican cooking.

CHOCOLATE

When the Spanish reached Mexico, they discovered a wealth of unfamiliar ingredients, including potatoes, vanilla, avocados and squash. One of their greatest finds, however, was chocolate. The Aztecs were very partial to a drink made from the beans of the cacao tree, which they flavoured in many different ways, and the Spanish, like the rest of the world after them, embraced this wonderful new taste with enthusiasm, developing a fondness for a variation that included corn, honey and spices.

The conquistadors took chocolate back to Spain, and it was not long before all the most fashionable resorts and cities in Europe boasted cocoa houses. Initially it was served as a drink, but Spanish women also prepared it as a sweetmeat, mixing it with sugar, cinnamon, eggs and almonds. Europeans started producing chocolate in slabs some two hundred years later, but women in Guatemala began pressing chocolate powder into bars for storage some time before this. When slabs of chocolate were finally produced in Mexico, the chocolate was sweetened and spiced in Spanish style.

Mexican Chocolate

This is made using dark and bitter chocolate mixed with sugar, ground nuts and cinnamon, and pressed into discs. The chocolate has a grainy quality, thanks to the sugar and almonds, and is crumbly when broken. One of the most popular brands is *Ibarra*, which comes in a distinctive yellow hexagonal box. Some specialist suppliers outside Mexico stock this product.

Buying and Storing

Mexican chocolate comes in packs, each containing five or six discs that are wrapped individually in waxed paper. Check the packet for a use-by date. Store in a cool, dry place.

Left: Ibarra chocolate

Making Mexican Chocolate

If you cannot buy Mexican chocolate, you can still make an acceptable substitute, using dark bitter chocolate with a minimum of 70 per cent cocoa solids.

Break 115g/4oz dark chocolate into pieces and put it in a food processor. Add 25g/1oz/¼ cup ground almonds, 50g/2oz/¼ cup caster sugar and 10ml/2 tsp ground cinnamon. Process to a fine powder, then tip into an airtight container, close the lid tightly and store in the fridge for up to 2 weeks, using as required.

Main Uses and Cooking Tips

The main use for chocolate in Mexico is still as a beverage. Mexicans are very partial to *Champurrada*, a chocolate corn drink, and the classic Mexican Hot Chocolate, which is whisked to a froth with a special whisk called a *molinollo*. Mexican Hot Chocolate is served with *Churros*, long fritters which are dunked in the drink, or *Pan Dulce*, the sweet bread that Mexicans eat for breakfast or as a snack late in the day. The extra ingredients make Mexican chocolate unsuitable for *moles*, the rich stews to which chocolate is traditionally added, so bitter chocolate or cocoa is used.

NUTS AND SEEDS

The three types of nut that are most widely used in Mexican cooking are the pecan, walnut and almond. Pine nuts are used in some desserts and pastries, and coconuts are valued both for their flesh and the cooling liquid they contain. Pecans grow in Northern Mexico. Walnuts, which were introduced from Europe, are cultivated in the colder, central highlands. The Spanish introduced almonds into Mexican cooking during the colonial era, but ensured that the trade with Spain was not disrupted by making it illegal for Mexicans themselves to cultivate them on a large scale.

Seeds from various types of pumpkin and squash have been important ingredients in Mexican cooking for centuries. At one time, pumpkins were grown mainly for their seeds; the flesh was discarded. Sesame seeds are also used, both in pastes and as a garnish on dishes such as *Mole Poblano*.

Buying and Storing

All types of nuts have a limited shelf life once they have been shelled. The oil in them quickly turns rancid, so they should only be bought as required, and stored in a cool, dry place for as short a time as possible. Nuts can, however, be frozen.

Main Uses and Cooking Tips

Salted or coated with sugar, pecans are eaten as a snack food, but their primary use is in desserts such as pecan cake. Almonds are used extensively, either whole, chopped or ground, in sweet and savoury dishes, including soups. Mexicans use ground almonds to thicken sauces, and substitute ground almonds for flour in some cakes and biscuits. Walnuts are also used in Mexican cooking, especially in biscuits, including *Polvorones de Nuez*, which are traditionally eaten at Christmas time (Christmas Cookies with Walnuts). Walnuts also feature in savoury dishes. Roasted salted pumpkin seeds are often served as snacks or an apetizer with drinks, while ground pumpkin seeds are used in sauces such as *Pepián*. Pine nuts, known as *piñon* seeds in Mexico, are added to dishes like *Picadillo* and are also ground for use in desserts and cakes.

Above: Pecans, almonds and walnuts

PILONCILLO – MEXICAN SUGAR

Mexico produces an unrefined brown cane sugar called *piloncillo*. It comes as small cones and adds a distinctive flavour and colour to any dish to which it is added. Unfortunately, *piloncillo* is still not readily available outside Mexico, but soft brown sugar can be used in recipes as a substitute.

Left: clockwise from top left: pumpkin seeds, sesame seeds and pine nuts

---

Roasting Seeds

When dry roasting or toasting pumpkin or sesame seeds, watch them carefully so that they do not burn. Use a heavy-based pan placed over a low heat, and stir or shake the pan frequently to keep the seeds on the move at all times. If they are allowed to burn, they will taste bitter and will spoil the flavour of any dish to which they are added.

FRUITS

Visit any Mexican market and what will strike you first are the colourful displays of fruit of every size, shape and colour. Some, such as mangoes, papayas and limes, will be familiar, but others may not look or taste like anything you have ever seen before. Fruit is an important part of the Mexican diet, providing the vitamins to balance the corn and beans that are the staple foods. Most of the fruit consumed in Mexico is grown in the country, and some of the surplus is exported to Europe.

CITRUS FRUIT

All types of citrus grow well in Mexico, and because the fruit is allowed to ripen naturally on the trees, it tends to have a very good flavour.

Description and Varieties

Limes have very thin skins which would eventually turn yellow if they were left on the tree long enough. The pulp is green and juicy. Mexican limes – limones – are smaller than other varieties. Almost round in shape, they taste very

Below: Lemons and limes

aromatic. **Lemons** are more oval, and have thicker skins with a dense layer of white pith just below the surface. Their pulp is yellow and acidic, but tastes markedly different to that of lime. **Oranges** grow well in Mexico and freshly squeezed orange juice is widely available, especially in the south. The fruits tend to look much paler than their brightly coloured counterparts in American markets, but are very sweet and juicy.

Buying and Storing

Mexican limes are seldom available outside the country, but any other type of lime can be substituted in recipes. Select limes with smooth, dark green skins, and avoid any that look wizened. The fruit should be heavy for its size. Small brown patches on the skin are harmless and will not affect the flavour or the juiciness of the fruit. Store uncut limes in a plastic bag in the fridge or a cool room. They will keep for up to 10 days in their peak condition. Lemons should be plump, with unblemished bright yellow skins. Avoid any whose skins are tinged with green, as this would indicate that the fruit is under-ripe. Oranges should feel heavy for their size. Avoid any that are damaged, shrivelled or have mouldy skins. Oranges keep well at room temperature.

Above: Oranges

Preparation

The rind on citrus fruit is often thinly pared or grated and used for decoration or flavouring. When paring the rind, take care to remove only the coloured outer layer, leaving the bitter white pith behind. The pith must be removed before the fruit is sliced or segmented.

Main Uses and Cooking Tips

Limes, lemons and oranges are used extensively in cooking. Both lime and lemon juice are used to preserve vegetables and are added to casseroles, fruit platters and fresh vegetable dishes to heighten the natural flavours. The most famous use of limes – other than with tequila – is in *Ceviche*. Raw fish or shellfish is marinated in the juice until the texture of the flesh changes, becoming as firm and white as if it had been cooked. Citrus juices are also used to prevent vegetables or fruits, such as avocados, from discolouring on contact with the air. The skins of oranges, lemons or limes are often ground, and the oil is used as a flavouring.

GRANADILLAS

These fruits are the largest members of the passion fruit family. Native to South America, they are round, with a small stalk attached at one end, so that they resemble Christmas tree baubles. The tough, shell-like outer skin is bright orange, while the pulp inside is green and very seedy. It smells and tastes like citrus fruit and is not as fragrant as the pulp of the smaller, purplish-black passion fruit.

Buying and Storing

Unlike passion fruit, which are wrinkled and dimpled when ripe, granadillas should be smooth, with no marks. They can be stored at room temperature for up to 1 week. When ripe, the pulp is moist and juicy, but it dries out if they are stored for too long.

Preparation

Cut the fruit in half and scoop out the pulp with a teaspoon. The seeds are edible, but sieve the pulp if you prefer.

Main Uses and Cooking Tips

Granadilla pulp can be used in desserts, either with the seeds, or sieved. It is often poured over ice cream or fruit salad, either on its own or in a dessert sauce. It also makes a superb fruit drink and the sieved pulp is often mixed with fresh orange juice.

Right: Granadillas

GUAVAS

These fruits – known as *guayabas* in Mexico – are native to the tropical areas of South America and grow in the warmer parts of Mexico. The guava tree grows to a height of about 10m/30ft and has smooth bark and fragrant white flowers. Guavas are an extremely good source of vitamin C. Purées or pastes made from the fruit have been popular in Mexico for centuries, and are still eaten today. They are either served alone or as accompaniments to fresh, soft cheeses.

Description

Guavas vary considerably in colour, shape and size. The variety most popular in Mexico is the yellow guava. When it is ripe the yellow guava has a slightly musky, not particularly pleasant smell. The skin is quite thick, and is referred to as the shell. Inside is a creamy pulp, which is full of edible seeds. The flesh has a clean, sweet, slightly acidic flavour.

Buying and Storing

Guavas should be bought when they are still firm and unblemished. You will find that under-ripe fruit will ripen quite quickly at room temperature. Ripe fruit, however, should be kept in a cool, dark place – or in the fridge – as guavas readily ferment and will soon become inedible.

Left: Guavas

Preparation

Cut the fruit in half and scrape out the flesh with a spoon. The seeds can be eaten, or the pulp can be pressed through a sieve if preferred.

Main Uses and Cooking Tips

Guavas are usually used in desserts, but their flavour is such that they are equally good in savoury dishes. Sweet guava sauces are served with cakes; savoury ones are excellent with fish.

In Mexico, guava flesh is often boiled with sugar, lemon juice, cinnamon and other spices to make a thick fruit purée. The purée is then poured into a shallow dish and left to cool, then cut into pieces to eat either on its own or with cheese. The fruit is also made into a preserve or relish.

Preparing a Mango

1 Place the mango narrow side down on a chopping board. Cut off a thick lengthways slice, keeping the knife as close to the stone as possible. Turn the mango round and repeat on the other side. Cut off the flesh adhering to the stone.

2 Score the flesh on each thick slice with criss-cross lines at 1cm/½in intervals, taking care not to cut through the skin.

3 Fold the mango halves inside out. The flesh will stand proud, in neat dice. Slice these off, or, for a "hedgehog", leave attached and serve.

MANGOES

Perhaps the most popular of all tropical fruits, mangoes have a wonderful perfume when ripe. The buttery flesh can be absolutely delicious, although some Mexican mangoes have a slightly resinous flavour.

Description and Varieties

There are thousands of varieties of mango. All start off green, but most will change to yellow, golden or red when they are ripe.

Buying and Storing

The best way of telling whether a mango is ripe is to sniff it. It should have a highly perfumed aroma. Next, press it lightly. If it is ripe, the fruit will just yield under your fingertips. Mangoes will ripen at home if placed in a paper bag with a banana. Eat them as soon as they are ripe.

Preparation

It has been said that the best way to eat a mango is in the bath. Failing that, use a sharp knife to take a lengthways slice off either side of the fruit, as close to the stone as possible. Scoop out the flesh from each slice, then cut the rest of the flesh off the stone so that none is wasted.

Main Uses and Cooking Tips

Mexicans love to eat ripe mangoes just as they are, after peeling them, but also use them in cooking, pureed in a range of desserts and fresh fruit drinks, with or without alcohol.

PINEAPPLES

Pineapples originated in South America and were introduced to other tropical areas by the Spanish and Portuguese. Historians have found records that prove that pineapples were cultivated by the indigenous peoples of Mexico long before the Spanish conquest.

Description and Varieties

Pineapples have hard, scaly skin and a crown of green leaves on top. The colour of the skin varies. Although most ripe pineapples are yellow or orange, some, such as the Sugar Loaf that grows in Mexico, are green when fully ripe. The flesh is yellow and very juicy, with a sweet flavour that can be tangy or even slightly tart.

Above: Mangoes

Main Uses and Cooking Tips

Mexican pineapples are deliciously sweet, and are usually served quite simply, as dessert. Pineapple is often combined with rice, in savoury dishes as well as sweet, and is used in puddings and sweetmeats. Pineapple juice is very popular, and is widely used in *agua frescas*, the fresh fruit drinks made at home and sold by street vendors.

Buying and Storing

Choose a pineapple that is slightly soft to touch, with a strong colour and crisp, green leaves.
Pineapples must be picked ripe as the starch doesn't convert to sugar after it has been picked.
Store in a fridge for up to 3 days.

Above: Pineapple

Preparing a Pineapple

1 Use a sharp knife to cut away the green leaves that form the crown and discard it.

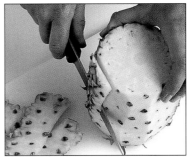

2 With a sharp knife, remove the skin from the pineapple cutting deeply enough to remove most of the "eyes".

3 Use a small knife to take out carefully any "eyes" that remain in the pineapple flesh.

4 Cut the pineapple lengthways into quarters and remove the core section from the centre of each piece. Chop the pineapple flesh or cut it into slices and use as required.

PRICKLY PEARS

Prickly pears are the fruits of several different types of cactus. Popular all over South America, they grow wild and are also cultivated, and serve as a staple food in some of the poorer rural areas of Mexico. The fleshy leaves of prickly pears – *nopales* – are treated as a vegetable, and you will find more information about them under the heading of Fruit Vegetables in the latter part of this introduction.

Description

Prickly pears are shaped like grenades and range in colour from deep red to greenish orange. Their name is well earned, for the tough outer skin has tiny tufts of hairs or prickles, which can be very sharp. The fruit is valued for its pulp, which has a sweet aromatic flavour, rather like that of melons, but even more subtle. The pulp contains small brown seeds, which are edible raw, but which become hard when cooked.

Right: Prickly pears

Buying and Storing

To tell whether a prickly pear is ripe, squeeze it carefully (avoiding the prickles!). Do not buy soft fruit or under-ripe fruit which is dark green in colour and very hard. Fruit that is slightly firm will ripen if left at room temperature for a few days.

Preparation

The prickles on these fruit are usually removed before they are sold, but if not, they can be scrubbed off with a stiff brush before the fruit is peeled. It is essential to wear kitchen gloves while carrying out this operation.

Main Uses and Cooking Tips

The peeled fruit should be halved and the flesh scooped out with a teaspoon. It can be strained and used as a sauce, or the fruit can be served as part of a fruit platter. Lime juice and chilli powder are sometimes added to enliven the flavour. Prickly pears can also be made into jelly or jam.

Peeling Prickly Pears

1 Having scrubbed off the prickles, put on a pair of kitchen gloves and hold the fruit down with one hand while you cut off the skin.

2 Alternatively, hold down the prickly pear with a fork and cut a thin slice from the top and bottom of the fruit, then slit the fruit from top to bottom on either side. Peel away the skin, then cut the flesh and arrange on a plate, or simply eat the pear whole.

3 If you prefer, cut the pear in half without removing the skin and scoop out the flesh with a teaspoon. You can eat the flesh in this way as you scoop, or transfer the pulp to a bowl and serve with lime juice.

Above: Coconut

Other Tropical Fruit Treats

Other fruits popular in Mexico include **papayas**, which are valued for the tenderizing qualities of their skins as well as delicious flesh. These pear-shaped fruits, with vivid yellow skins, are also used in drinks sold by street vendors to quench commuters' thirsts on hot afternoons. Mexicans eat fruit with ground chillies and lime juice as a snack, or part of a meal and slices of papaya are often included. The peppery, round black seeds are edible but are seldom used in dishes.

Pomegranates, which are used in sauces including the famous dish of *Chiles en Nagada*, which is often prepared for special occasions. Pomegranates are also used in refreshing drinks called *Agua Frescas* sold by street vendors. Be careful only to use the seeds and not the bitter-tasting white pith. **Sapodillas** have luscious honey-coloured flesh and taste like vanilla-flavoured banana custard.

Coconuts are grown in parts of Mexico and pieces are often sold from bowls, cooled with iced water on street corners in busy towns. A chilled coconut soup is often made in the northern Pacific areas. One of the most popular fruits in Mexico is the **sapote**, it is which has dark salmon-pink flesh. It is very sweet and rather cloying, but makes excellent marmalade, which accounts for its alternative name of marmalade plum.

Above: Papayas

Preparing a Pomegranate

1 Cut off a thin slice from one end.

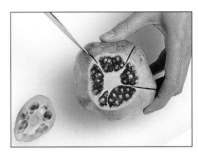

2 Stand the fruit upright. Cut downwards through the skin at intervals, using a small sharp knife.

3 Bend back the segments and use your fingers to push the seeds into a bowl.

4 Remove all the bitter pith and membrane and use as required.

FRUIT VEGETABLES

There are some fruits which are used so often in savoury dishes that we tend to think of them as vegetables. Tomatoes are the obvious example, but avocados, peppers and chillies also come into this category. Mexico seems to have more than its fair share of these fruit vegetables, including the tomatillo, which is often called the Mexican green tomato, although it is actually related to the physalis.

AVOCADOS

It is believed that the Aztecs introduced avocado seedlings to Mexico during the 13th and 14th centuries, calling them *ahuacatl*, a name whose Spanish version was first corrupted to alligator pear and then to the name by which the fruit vegetable is known today.

Description and Varieties

There are several varieties of avocado. Most are pear-shaped and contain a central stone. The flesh ranges in colour from creamy yellow to bright green and has a buttery texture and mild but distinctive flavour.

The indigenous Mexican avocado has fragrant green flesh around a large stone. The thin skin can be eaten, which is unusual, since most avocados have skins that are tough and inedible, and some, like the Hass variety, have

Left: Avocado

knobbly black skins that are almost shell-like. Hass avocados have creamy flesh and a very good flavour. Another variety is the fuerte avocado, which has glossy green skin and yellow-green flesh.

Buying and Storing

To confirm that an avocado is ripe, press the top end of the fruit gently. It should just yield. If it is soft, the fruit is over-ripe, will prove messy to peel and will have flesh that is soft and mushy. Avocados that are bruised will have blackened flesh.

Finding the perfect avocado is partly a matter of luck, however. Even if you have chosen carefully and have taken great care not to let the fruit get bruised on the journey from the shop to your home, the flesh may still be flecked with brownish spots when you finally cut it open.

Store ripe avocados in the fridge; under-ripe fruit will ripen if left for a few days in a warm room. Cut avocados discolour quickly. Although this process can be delayed slightly, it is much more advisable not to prepare the fruit until you are ready to serve it.

Main Uses and Cooking Tips

Avocados are used extensively in Mexican cookery, most famously in Guacamole, the mashed avocado dip. They are also used in soups – both hot and cold – or to make a hot sauce for meat. Fresh avocado tastes wonderful in salads and with seafood. It is often used in tortilla dishes and is also a favourite ingredient in a range of *tortas* – Mexican sandwiches.

As soon as an avocado is cut, the flesh begins to blacken. Sprinkling the slices or chunks with lemon or lime juice delays the process somewhat, and Mexicans swear that burying the avocado stone in the mashed avocado flesh has the same effect.

Avocado Leaves

In Mexico and other countries where the fruit flourishes, fresh or dried avocado leaves are used for their flavouring properties, much as bay leaves are used elsewhere. They can either be crushed and added to dishes or put in whole and then removed just before the dish is served. Dried avocado leaves are usually toasted before being added to dishes such as Refried Beans, stews and marinades, or used for meat that is going to be grilled or barbecued.

Guacamole

Guacamole originated in Mexico, but has become one of the world's most popular dishes. Mashed avocado is the main ingredient, but other items, such as onion, garlic, diced tomato, chopped chillies, lime or lemon juice as well as seasonings are added. The smooth, buttery taste of the avocado gives this dip a creamy texture, yet it contains no saturated fat. Guacamole is often served with tortilla chips as a simple dip. It is an essential accompaniment to fajitas, is used in *tortas*, and is served alongside meat and fish dishes.

Simple Guacamole

1 Cut two avocados in half. Remove the stones and scoop the flesh out of the shells. Place it in a blender and process until almost smooth. Transfer into a bowl and add the juice of half a lime.

2 Add one-quarter of a small onion, chopped finely, a crushed garlic clove and a handful of fresh coriander, also chopped finely.

3 Add salt and other seasoning to taste and serve immediately, with tortilla chips for dipping. The Guacamole will keep in the fridge for 2–3 days if it is kept in an airtight container.

VARIATION

Try adding chopped fresh tomatoes and fresh chilli to give your Guacamole added flavour, texture and fire.

Preparing Avocado

1 If a recipe calls for avocado halves or mashed avocado, run a small, sharp knife all the way around the fruit, starting at the top and cutting right in until the knife touches the stone.

2 Gently prise the two halves apart with the knife.

3 Push the knife blade into the stone, then lift it away. If any of the brown skin from the stone remains on the avocado flesh, remove it. The avocado halves can be served with vinaigrette, filled with prawns or topped with thin slices of ham. Alternatively, the flesh can be scooped into a bowl and mashed.

1 For avocado slices, cut the fruit in half, remove the stone, then nick the skin at the top of each half and ease it away until you can peel away the skin completely; if the avocado is ripe, it will come away cleanly and easily.

2 Cut the peeled avocado halves into slices, leaving them attached at one end if you want to fan them on the plate. Sprinkle them with lemon or lime juice to stop them from discolouring too quickly.

1 For cubes of avocado, score the half of avocado and then with the tip of the knife gently lift each cube out one by one.

Left: Tomatoes

TOMATOES

Tomatoes are native to western South America and were cultivated by the Aztecs long before the Spanish invasion. Hernando Cortés is credited with introducing the first tomatoes – yellow ones – to Europe. They were initially treated with suspicion, but after a pair of Jesuit priests introduced red tomatoes to Italy in the 18th century, they steadily become more and more popular.

Description and Varieties

There are numerous varieties of tomato, ranging from tiny cherry tomatoes to ridged beefsteak tomatoes that measure as much as 10cm/4in across. Great piles of plum tomatoes are a common sight in Mexican markets. Richly flavoured, with fewer seeds than most other varieties, they are a popular choice for salads and salsas.

Buying and Storing

Tomatoes sold in Mexican markets will have ripened naturally, and will be full of flavour, so use ripe home-grown tomatoes or vine tomatoes when cooking Mexican dishes. Over-ripe tomatoes can be used for soups or purées, but avoid any tomatoes which show signs of mould. Avoid buying tomatoes that are still green, but pale ones that have begun to redden can be ripened in a brown paper bag, especially if you add a slice of apple. Try to either store fresh tomatoes at room temperature, or bring them to room temperature before use, as chilling dulls the flavour.

Preparation

If a recipe requires that a tomato be seeded, just cut it in half and squeeze gently, or scoop out the seeds with a teaspoon. To peel, cut a cross in the base of the tomato, immerse it in boiling water for 3 minutes, then plunge into cold water. Drain well. The skins will have begun to peel back from the crosses and will be easy to remove. Chop or slice the tomatoes, as required in individual recipes. If sliced tomatoes are called for, it is better to slice them across, rather than downwards.

Main Uses and Cooking Tips

Mexicans use tomatoes in so many of their recipes that it would be impossible to list them all. They feature in both hot and cold soups, salsas, salads and meat and fish dishes. Chopped tomatoes are added to beans to make *frijoles*, are mixed with avocados in Guacamole, and are used in Sangrita, a popular drink that is sipped alternately with tequila.

Quick Fresh Tomato Salsa
A quick and easy tomato salsa, which can be prepared in minutes. Serve as a side dish with meat or fish, or as a simple starter with a pile of tortilla chips.

INGREDIENTS
3 fresh tomatoes, chopped
1 red onion, finely chopped
1 clove of garlic, crushed
½ green pepper, finely chopped
15ml/1 tbsp chopped jalapeño or fresno chilli, finely chopped
30ml/2 tbsp chopped coriander
45ml/3 tbsp fresh lime juice
salt and ground black pepper to taste

1 Place the tomatoes, onion, garlic, green pepper and chilli in a large bowl and mix together.

2 Add the chopped coriander and fresh lime juice, then taste and season with salt and ground black pepper to taste. Serve immediately or transfer to an airtight container and store in the fridge.

TOMATILLOS/TOMATE VERDE

Despite the name by which we know them – and the fact that they are sometimes referred to as Mexican green tomatoes – tomatillos are not members of the tomato family. Instead, they are related to physalis, those pretty little orange fruit surrounded by papery lanterns, which are so popular for garnishing. They have been grown in Mexico since Aztec times, when they were known as *miltomatl*. Mexicans seldom use the term "tomatillo", preferring to call these fruit by one of their many local names, which include *fresadilla* and *tomate milpero*.

Description

Ranging in colour from yellowish green to lime, tomatillos are firm, round fruit, about the size of a small tomato, but lighter in weight, as they are not juicy. Fresh ones usually have the brown

Left: Tomatillos with husks

papery husk attached to them at the stem end. The flavour resembles that of tart apples with a hint of lemon, and is enhanced by cooking, although a *salsa cruda* of raw tomatillos has a very pleasant, clean taste.

Buying and Storing

Fresh tomatillos are difficult to come by outside Mexico, but some specialist stores sell them, and they are also available by mail order in season. They can also be grown from seed, a most worthwhile enterprise for anyone who loves their clean, slightly acidic flavour. If you do locate a supply of fresh tomatillos, look for firm fruit with tight-fitting husks, and store them in the fridge for up to 1 week.

In the same way that canned carrots bear little resemblance to fresh ones, canned tomatillos are softer and not as tasty as fresh, but they are more readily available and preferable to missing out on this great flavour completely. When buying canned tomatillos, be sure to take account of the loss of weight when the liquid is drained off – it can be as much as a third of the total.

Main Uses and Cooking Tips

Tomatillos are used in table salsas and in the sauce (*tomate verde salsa*) which is poured over enchiladas before they are cooked. They can also be used instead of tomatoes in Guacamole, giving a piquant flavour to the sauce. To cook fresh tomatillos, remove the husks and dry fry them in a heavy-based frying pan until the skins have begun to char and the flesh has softened. Alternatively, put them in a pan with water to cover, bring to the boil, then simmer them until they soften and begin to break down. If the dish in which they are used requires stock, use the cooking liquid.

Above: Canned tomatillos

Salsa Cruda de Tomatillo

1 To make a rough textured salsa with tomatillos, process 450g/1lb raw tomatillos in a food processor or chop them finely, then mix with one chopped small onion and one crushed garlic clove. Add two seeded and chopped jalapeño chillies and salt to taste.

2 Finely chop a small bunch of fresh coriander and add it to the tomatillo mixture.

3 Stir well, spoon into a clean bowl and serve at once with freshly made corn tortilla chips.

Right: Plantains

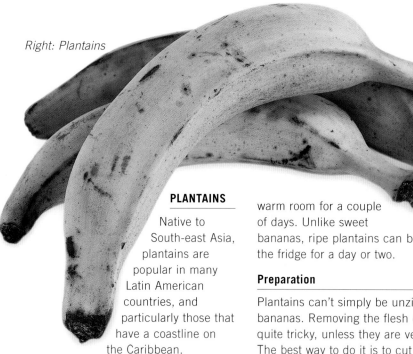

PLANTAINS

Native to South-east Asia, plantains are popular in many Latin American countries, and particularly those that have a coastline on the Caribbean.

Description and Varieties

Plantains are a type of banana, larger than the sweet bananas and with a harder skin. There are several varieties, all initially green, but some ripening to yellow, then black, while others become dark pink or red when ripe. The flesh is fibrous and starchy and must be cooked before being eaten. The flavour can be quite mild, resembling that of a squash, but when plantains are fried, the flesh tastes sweeter and has a more obvious banana flavour.

Buying and Storing

Both green and ripe plantains are used in cooking. Look for them in markets specializing in West Indian or African foods. Ripe plantains are slightly soft to the touch. If a recipe calls for ripe plantains, and you can only get green or yellow ones, they will ripen if left in a warm room for a couple of days. Unlike sweet bananas, ripe plantains can be stored in the fridge for a day or two.

Preparation

Plantains can't simply be unzipped, like bananas. Removing the flesh can be quite tricky, unless they are very ripe. The best way to do it is to cut the plantains into short lengths, then slit the skin along one of the natural ridges so that it can be eased apart and removed. Unless you are going to use the peeled plantains immediately, put them in a bowl of acidulated water (water to which lime juice has been added) to prevent them from discolouring. When slicing plantains for chips, don't remove the skins first. Put the slices into a bowl of salted water for about half an hour, then drain them. It will be quite easy to press the slices of plantain out of their skins.

Main Uses and Cooking Tips

Plantains are used in both sweet and savoury dishes. Fried plantain slices are delicious with a chilli dip or simply a squeeze of lime and a sprinkling of chilli powder. Slices can be cooked in butter and served as a vegetable, the sweet creaminess making them a good partner for a hot, spicy dish. They are good in meat dishes, but make a delectable dessert. Just cook them in butter and cinnamon, with a little sugar and a good measure of rum.

Right: Sweet peppers

Banana Leaves

In parts of Mexico, banana leaves are used instead of corn husks for wrapping food before cooking. Before use, the leaves should be soaked in water until soft, then dried on kitchen paper. They will impart a unique, slightly lemony flavour to food cooked in them.

SWEET PEPPERS

Sometimes known as bell peppers or capsicums, these are native to Mexico and Central America, and were also a staple food for the Incas in Peru.

Description

Sweet peppers range in colour from green through yellow and orange to deep red, depending on ripeness, and there is even a purplish-black variety. They have a mild, sweet flavour and crisp, juicy flesh. Peppers can be eaten raw or cooked.

Buying and Storing

When buying peppers, try to look for specimens with bright, glossy skins. Avoid any that are limp or wrinkled, or that have "blistered" areas on the skin. Store them in a cool place or in the fridge for up to 1 week.

Preparation

Inside each pepper is a core that is surrounded by seeds, which must be removed. If the peppers are to be used whole, this can be lifted out if a neat slice is taken off the top, around the stem. If the peppers are halved or quartered, removing the core and seeds is even easier. Many Mexican recipes call for peppers to be roasted over a gas

Right: Nopales

flame or in a dry frying pan, then sealed in a plastic bag until the steam loosens the skin, which is removed before the peppers are sliced or chopped.

Main Uses and Cooking Tips

Peppers are used extensively in Mexican cuisine, contributing colour and flavour to salsas, stews and meat fillings, as well as fish dishes, vegetable medleys and salads. For salads, they are usually just cored, seeded and chopped, but for cooked dishes, it is more usual for them to be roasted and skinned first.

NOPALES

Nopales are the edible leaves of several varieties of prickly pear cactus. Fat and fleshy, they are often called cactus paddles. Mexicans have been cooking and eating them for thousands of years.

Description

The leaves – or paddles – are oval in shape, with sharp spines. They range in colour from pale to dark green, depending on variety and age. The flavour is similar to that of a green bean, but with a slightly acidic tang.

Buying and Storing

Fresh *nopales* are quite difficult to locate outside Mexico and the adjoining American states. If you do find them, choose the thinnest, smallest leaves with the palest colour, as older leaves can be very woody, even when cooked. Store fresh *nopales* in the fridge for up to 1 week. Bottled *nopales* – called *nopalitos* – have had the spines removed and are sliced before being preserved in brine or vinegar. They are available from specialist food shops.

Preparing Peppers

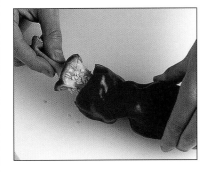

1 For peppers to be served whole, use a sharp knife to cut a ring around the stem at the top of each pepper. Lift out the core and surrounding seeds. If the peppers can be cut into halves or quarters, do this taking care not to cut into the core, then cut around it and remove.

2 For roasted peppers, roast over a gas flame or in a dry frying pan or griddle.

3 Place them in a strong plastic bag and seal the bag. Leave until the steam loosens the skin. Remove the skin and slice or chop the peppers.

Preparing *Nopales*

1 Wearing gloves or holding each paddle in turn with kitchen tongs, cut off the bumps that contain the thorns with a sharp knife. Try not to remove the whole of the green outer surface; just the parts containing spines.

2 Cut off and discard the thick base from each paddle. Rinse the paddles well and either chop them or cut them into strips.

Main Uses

Nopales are used in stews and soups, particularly in the Tlaxcala area of Mexico, and are pickled for use in salsas and salad dishes. They are even added to scrambled eggs.

Cooking Nopales

Cactus can be slimy when cooked. Mexican cooks often add onion and garlic at the start of cooking, removing them after the sliminess has gone. You can also boil *nopales* in water, drain them, then rinse under cold water. Cover with a damp dish towel and leave for 30 minutes, by which time the gumminess will have disappeared.

CHILLIES

Chillies have been grown in South America for thousands of years. Over 150 indigenous varieties are found in Mexico alone. In 1942 Columbus brought chillies to Europe, and from there they spread around the world.

Mexican food is often perceived as being very hot, and some of the dishes certainly live up to their reputation, but it is possible to find many dishes that are only mildly flavoured with chillies. The heat level of a chilli is determined by the amount of capsaicin it contains. This compound is concentrated mainly in the ribs and seeds, so you can reduce the fieriness considerably by removing these parts. Chillies that have been pickled, or that are used raw, tend to have more heat than cooked chillies.

Below: Jalapeño and serrano chillies

Left: Poblana chillies

The heat level of a chilli is measured in Scoville units, on a scale where 0 is the heat level of a sweet pepper and 300,000 is the hottest chilli, the habañero. In many instances, the ratings have been simplified to a scale of 1–10, to make them easier to remember.

The heat level of a particular chilli will vary according to where it was grown, when it was picked, the irrigation, the weather during the growing season and a host of other factors, so Scoville units can only be a guide. Each crop from the same plant will be different.

Fresh Chillies

The following are the most commonly used fresh chillies:

Serrano Heat level 8. This is a small chilli, about 4–5cm/1½–2in long and 1cm/½in wide, with a pointed tip. Serrano chillies change from green to red when ripe, and are sold at both stages of their development. The flavour is clean and biting. Serranos are used in cooked dishes, Guacamole and salsas.

Jalapeño Heat level 6. One of the most common – and most popular – types of chilli, this is about the same length as a serrano, but plumper. Jalapeños are sold at all stages of ripeness, so you are as likely to find red as green. Green jalapeños are often pickled. One method of preparing jalapeños is to stuff with fresh cheese, coat in a light batter and deep fry.

Poblano Heat level 3. Like many chillies, poblanos are initially green, and ripen to a dark red. They are large chillies, being roughly 8cm/3½in long

Roasting and Peeling Chillies

1 Dry fry the chillies in a frying pan or griddle until the skins are scorched. Alternatively, spear them on a long-handled metal skewer and roast them over the flame of a gas burner until the skins blister and darken. Do not let the flesh burn.

2 Place the roasted chillies in a strong plastic bag and tie the top to keep the steam in. Set aside for 20 minutes.

3 Remove the chillies from the bag and peel off the skins. Cut off the stalks, then slit the chillies and scrape out the seeds.

Above: Fresno chillies

and 5.5cm/2¼in wide, and are sometimes said to be heart-shaped. Although not very hot, poblanos have a rich, earthy flavour which is intensified when the chillies are roasted and peeled. They are widely used in Mexican cooking, notably in Stuffed Chillies (*Chiles Rellenos*). Anaheim chillies, which are widely available in the United States and sometimes in the UK, can be substituted for poblanos.

Fresno Heat level 8. Looking rather like elongated sweet peppers, fresnos are about 6cm/2½in long and 2cm/¾in wide. They have a hot, sweet flavour and are used in salsas, as well as in meat, fish and vegetable dishes. Fresno chillies are particularly good when added to Guacamole.

Buying and Storing Fresh Chillies

Look for firm fresh chillies, with shiny skins. Try to avoid any specimens that are dull or limp, as they will be past their best. Fresh chillies can be successfully stored in a plastic bag in the fridge for up to 3 weeks. If they are to be chopped and added to cooked dishes, they can be seeded, chopped and then frozen, ready for use until required.

COOK'S TIP

If you bite into a chilli that is uncomfortably hot, swallow a spoonful of sugar. Don't be tempted to gulp down a glass of water or beer; this will only spread the heat further.

Preparing Fresh Chillies

Be very careful when handling fresh chillies as the capsaicin that they contain can cause severe irritation to sensitive skin, especially on the face. Either wear gloves when working with them, or wash your hands thoroughly with soap after handling them. If you touch your skin by mistake, wash your hands quickly and then splash the affected area with plenty of fresh cold water. Avoid scratching or rubbing enflamed skin, as this could aggravate the problem.

1 Holding the chilli firmly at the stalk end, cut it in half lengthwise with a sharp knife.

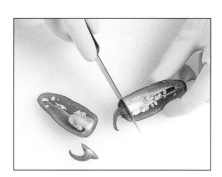

2 Cut off the stalk from both halves of the chilli, removing a thin slice of the top of the chilli as you do so. This will help to free the white membrane and make it easier to scrape out.

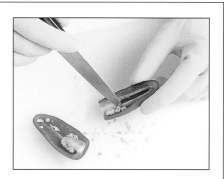

3 Carefully scrape out all of the seeds and remove the core with a small sharp knife.

4 Cut out any white membrane from the inside of the chillies. Keep the knife close to the flesh so that all the membrane is removed.

5 At this point make sure you carefully discard all of the seeds and membrane that are now lying on the board. Then take each half chilli and cut as required. To chop finely first cut the chilli half into thin strips. Then bunch the strips together and cut across them to produce tiny pieces. If the chilli is being added to a dish that will be cooked for some time you can chop it less finely.

DRIED CHILLIES

Dried chillies are nothing new. The convenience of a product that could be stored and rehydrated when needed was realised centuries ago. Chillies were originally sun-dried, but today are more likely to be dried in an oven. Either way, they are a valuable ingredient, and are extensively used in this book because they are so much easier to obtain than fresh chillies are.

In many cases, drying intensifies the flavour of chillies. Depending on the process used, drying can also impart extra flavour, as when jalapeños are dried and smoked. Not only does the flavour deepen to a rich smokiness, but the name of the chilli changes, and it becomes a chipotle. The fact that the same chilli can have two names,

Above: Chilli powder

Above: Ancho chillies

Below: Cascabel chillies

depending on whether it is fresh or dried, can be confusing, and it may be simpler to think of dried chillies as separate varieties. The heat rating given for the dried chillies in the list that follows is based on the same scale as that used for the fresh chillies on the previous pages. Drying seems to spread the capsaicin through the chillies, so removing the seeds and membrane will do little to alter their heat. The seeds of a dried chilli add very little to the flavour, however, so if they are loose, discard them. Dried chillies can be ground to a powder or cut into strips before being used. Unless the chillies are to be added to a dish with a high proportion of liquid, they are usually soaked in water before use.

Buying and Storing Dried Chillies

Good quality dried chillies should be flexible, not brittle. Store them in an airtight jar in a cool, dry place. For short term storage, the fridge is ideal, although they can also be frozen. Do not keep dried chillies for more than a year or the flavour may depreciate.

The following is a list of some of the more common dried chillies

Ancho Heat scale 3. The most common dried chilli in Mexico, the ancho is a dried red poblano chilli, and has a fruity, slightly sharp flavour. When rehydrated, anchos can be used to make Stuffed Chillies (*Chiles Rellenos*), but should not be peeled first.
Cascabel Heat scale 4. The name means "little rattle" and refers to the noise that the seeds make inside the chilli. This chilli has a chocolate brown skin, and

Right: Chipotle chillies

Grinding Chillies

This method gives a distinctive and smoky taste to the resulting chilli powder.

1 Soak the chillies, pat dry and then dry fry in a heavy-based pan until crisp.

2 Transfer to a mortar and grind to a fine powder with a pestle. Store in an airtight container.

remains dark, even after soaking. Cascabels have a slightly nutty flavour and are often added to salsas such as *tomate verde.*
Chipotle Heat scale 6. These are smoked jalapeños. They add a

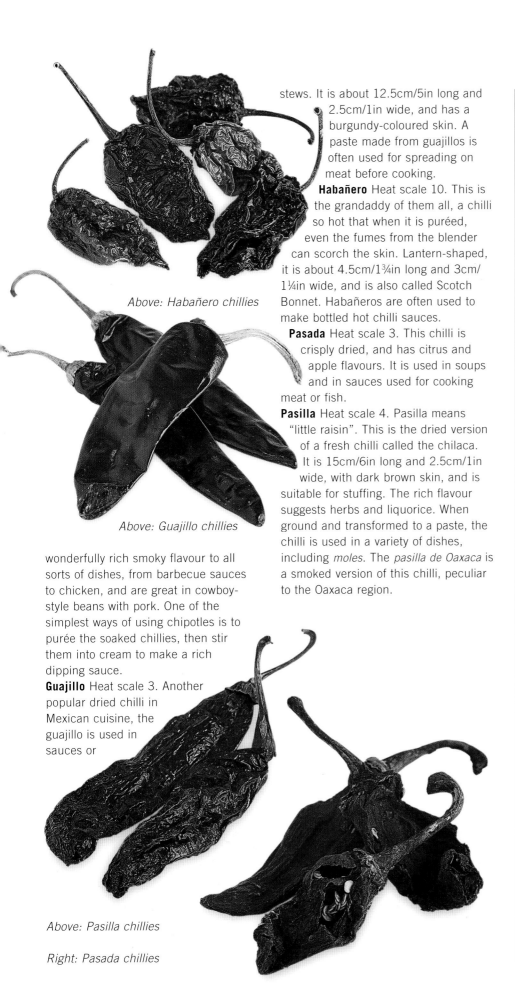

Above: Habañero chillies

Above: Guajillo chillies

stews. It is about 12.5cm/5in long and 2.5cm/1in wide, and has a burgundy-coloured skin. A paste made from guajillos is often used for spreading on meat before cooking.

Habañero Heat scale 10. This is the grandaddy of them all, a chilli so hot that when it is puréed, even the fumes from the blender can scorch the skin. Lantern-shaped, it is about 4.5cm/1¾in long and 3cm/1¼in wide, and is also called Scotch Bonnet. Habañeros are often used to make bottled hot chilli sauces.

Pasada Heat scale 3. This chilli is crisply dried, and has citrus and apple flavours. It is used in soups and in sauces used for cooking meat or fish.

Pasilla Heat scale 4. Pasilla means "little raisin". This is the dried version of a fresh chilli called the chilaca. It is 15cm/6in long and 2.5cm/1in wide, with dark brown skin, and is suitable for stuffing. The rich flavour suggests herbs and liquorice. When ground and transformed to a paste, the chilli is used in a variety of dishes, including *moles*. The *pasilla de Oaxaca* is a smoked version of this chilli, peculiar to the Oaxaca region.

wonderfully rich smoky flavour to all sorts of dishes, from barbecue sauces to chicken, and are great in cowboy-style beans with pork. One of the simplest ways of using chipotles is to purée the soaked chillies, then stir them into cream to make a rich dipping sauce.

Guajillo Heat scale 3. Another popular dried chilli in Mexican cuisine, the guajillo is used in sauces or

Above: Pasilla chillies

Right: Pasada chillies

Soaking Dried Chillies

In order to appreciate their full flavour, it is recommended that dried chillies which are not being ground should be soaked before being used. The amount of time chillies need to rehydrate depends on the type, the thickness of the skin and how dry they are. The longer they soak the better, so if there is time, leave them in the water for 1 hour before cooking.

1 Wipe them to remove any dirt, and brush away any seeds that are accessible.

2 Soak the dried chillies in a bowl of hot water for about 10 minutes (longer if possible) until the colour is restored and the chilli has swelled and softened.

3 Drain, cut off the stalks, then slit the chillies and scrape out the seeds with a small sharp knife. Slice or chop the flesh. If the chillies are to be puréed, put them in a blender or food processor with a little of the soaking water and process them until smooth.

VEGETABLES

Mexico's indigenous peoples were very good agriculturists, and when the Spanish invaded they found a country blessed with abundant vegetables, including corn (maize), sweet potatoes, *jicama*, pumpkins and courgettes. The Spanish in turn introduced onions, garlic, green beans, cabbage and cauliflower, all of which were integrated into the Mexican cuisine.

CORN (MAIZE)

The vegetable we know as sweetcorn has been grown in the Americas for over five thousand years. It was brought to Europe by the Spanish in the late 15th century, but long before that it was a staple food of the indigenous peoples of Mexico, who used every part of the corn, including the husks and silks.

Description

An ear of corn consists of yellow, plump kernels on a firm cob, sheathed in long green leaves or husks. Between the leaves and the kernels are long thin threads called silks. Mexicans traditionally use these for tying *tamales*, but elsewhere they are usually discarded.

Buying and Storing

Look for ears whose outer leaves are a fresh, tender green. They should not be limp or faded. One way of testing whether the corn is fresh is to squeeze one of the kernels gently. A milky liquid should ooze out. Sweetcorn should be cooked within 24 hours of being purchased, because the sugar starts turning to starch the moment it is cut. The older the sweetcorn, the less sweet it will be.

Preparation

Peel off the husks, then pull off the silks. (If necessary, scrub the cobs with a vegetable brush to remove any remaining silks.) If the sweetcorn is to be cooked on the barbecue, the husks can be pulled back, then replaced after removing the silks.

Main Uses and Cooking Tips

Corn cobs can be cooked in boiling water, but do not add salt or the kernels will toughen. They can also be cooked in the oven or on the barbecue. In Mexico, sweetcorn is a popular street food. The cooked cobs are dipped in cream,

Above: Corn

then sprinkled with cheese. A similar dish involves removing the kernels from the cobs and cooking them in cream with pickled jalapeños and cheese.

Above: Beans

GREEN BEANS

Green beans have been growing in the Americas for hundreds of years. In Mexico lima beans, sometimes called fava beans, are widely used, as are French or string beans.

Buying and Storing

Beans pods should be bright and crisp. Use on the day bought if possible.

Preparation

Top and tail the beans (cut off both ends) and remove any strings on the sides of the pods. Lima beans and broad beans must be removed from their soft, fleshy pods before use, and are sometimes blanched.

Main Uses and Cooking Tips

Mexicans use beans in salads and vegetable dishes. A favourite dish is lima beans with a tomato sauce. Beans are best cooked briefly in boiling water, or steamed until they are tender. Both these methods ensure the beans retain maximum colour, texture and flavour.

Right: Sweet potatoes

SWEET POTATOES

One of the staple foods of the indigenous peoples of Mexico in pre-Columbian times, sweet potatoes are still a very important food.

Description and Varieties

Sweet potatoes are starchy tubers, and need to be cooked before being eaten. There are many different varieties, ranging from pale-skinned sweet potatoes with pale crumbly flesh to darker tubers with thick skins and moist flesh. The skin colour can be anything from pink to deep purple, and the flesh can range from creamy white to the more familiar vivid orange. As their name suggests, they have a sweet flavour, but with a hint of spice.

Buying and Storing

Sweet potatoes have smooth skins and should not be damaged or soft. Smaller specimens often have finer flavour than large ones. They can be stored in a cool, dark place for up to 1 week.

Preparation

Cook sweet potatoes in their skins, or, if you prefer, peel them just before boiling and mashing them.

Main Uses and Cooking Tips

Sweet potatoes are used in both sweet and savoury dishes, either cooked slowly in their skins or peeled and boiled. Try them boiled and mashed with a little butter and cream, and some nutmeg, salt and black pepper. A sweet potato mash, with tomatoes and chillies, is a wonderful accompaniment to barbecued food. Roast sweet potatoes are excellent with roast pork. They are also used in stews and casseroles.

Below: Jicamas

JICAMAS

The *jicama* – or yam bean – is a native of Central America. It was introduced to the Philippines by the Spanish, and from there it spread to China, where it is still popular today. In fact, Chinese supermarkets are a good source of *jicama*. The Chinese name for it is *saa got*, but you may also find it labelled Chinese turnip.

Description

Jicama is the root of a climbing bean plant. The young beans are edible, but older ones are poisonous. It looks like a turnip or beetroot, but has a conical base. The skin is light brown and quite thin. The moist, creamy-coloured flesh tastes slightly fruity, and the texture resembles that of a crisp green apple or a water chestnut. *Jicama* can be eaten raw or cooked.

Buying and Storing

Look for firm *jicamas* that are about the size of a large turnip; larger ones may be a bit woody. To keep the crisp texture, store them in the fridge for up to 1 week.

Preparation

Peel away the thin, papery skin by hand or with a sharp knife, then slice the *jicama* thinly.

Main Uses and Cooking Tips

Raw *jicama* makes a refreshing snack when it is sprinkled with freshly squeezed orange juice and served with chilli powder and salt. It is also delicious added to salads and used in salsas. *Jicama* retains its pleasingly crisp texture when boiled, as long as it is not overcooked. Mexicans sometimes like to use grated *jicama* in desserts.

SQUASH

Pumpkins and other types of squash, cucumbers and *chayotes* all belong to the same family, and have been cultivated since ancient times. Pumpkin seeds dating back as far as 7000BC have been found in Mexico. The word "squash" comes from an Indian word, "askutasquash" meaning raw or uncooked, which may seem odd to those of us accustomed to eating squash cooked. However, there are numerous types of squash, and some are indeed delicious eaten raw.

Description

There are two main classifications of squash – summer and winter. Many of the summer squash are now available all the year round, but it can still be useful to differentiate between the two distinct groups.

Summer squash grow on bushes and have thin, edible skins and soft seeds. Examples include courgettes, patty pans and vegetable marrows. The flesh

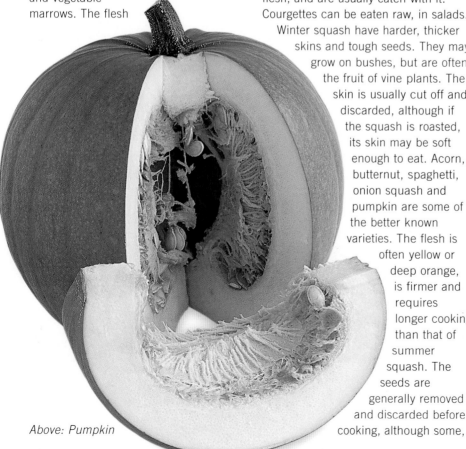

Above: Summer squash

is soft, generally pale in colour and has a high water content. It only needs a little cooking, and has a mild flavour. The seeds are dispersed through the flesh, and are usually eaten with it. Courgettes can be eaten raw, in salads.

Winter squash have harder, thicker skins and tough seeds. They may grow on bushes, but are often the fruit of vine plants. The skin is usually cut off and discarded, although if the squash is roasted, its skin may be soft enough to eat. Acorn, butternut, spaghetti, onion squash and pumpkin are some of the better known varieties. The flesh is often yellow or deep orange, is firmer and requires longer cooking than that of summer squash. The seeds are generally removed and discarded before cooking, although some,

Above: Pumpkin

such as pumpkin seeds, are a valuable food in their own right.

The blossoms or flowers from both winter and summer squash are edible, and there are a number of Mexican recipes for cooking squash blossoms. In Mexico you can buy the blossoms separately, and they are sold in some speciality food shops elsewhere, but most cooks who want to try them will have to harvest them from home-grown vegetables. They are delicious coated in light batter and fried.

Buying and Storing

Summer squash, and courgettes in particular, are best when they are small, slim and still tender. They should have bright, smooth, unblemished skins with no bruising. They should be stored in the fridge, and will only keep for 3–4 days. The thicker skins of winter squash make them much better keepers. They can be stored in a cool room for up to 1 month, depending on how mature they were when picked and on how old they were when sold. When buying winter squash, choose specimens that are heavy for their size and that have unmarked skins.

Main Uses and Cooking Tips

Summer squash comes in a variety of shapes, sizes and colours, and can be steamed, stir-fried, boiled, baked or even coated in batter and deep fried. As the flesh is soft, it will only need to be cooked for a few minutes and should still retain some bite.

Winter squash are often cut into pieces, seeded and baked, steamed or boiled. They need to be cooked for longer than summer squash because the flesh is firmer. The skin is usually discarded, and this can be done either before cooking or after.

Mexicans often roast pumpkins in large chunks. They also cook pumpkin in water and sugar, as a dessert, or bake it with sugar and spices in the oven. Other types of squash are used in similar ways, and cooked squash often features as a filling in both sweet and savoury

empanadas.

CHAYOTES

The *chayote* is native to Mexico. A member of the squash family, it grows on a vine, and goes under several names, including vegetable pear, *chocho* or *chow-chow*, *mirliton* and *choko*. In France it is called a *christophene*.

Chayotes are pale green and pear-shaped, with smooth and leathery skins, which are often furrowed and may be covered with short spines. Inside is a large, flat seed, similar in appearance to that found in a mango. *Chayote* seeds are, however, edible. The flesh is pale and crisp, like that of a tart green apple or a water chestnut.

Buying and Storing

Choose a firm *chayote* with a smooth, unwrinkled skin that is free from blemishes or bruising. Smaller

Left: Chayote

chayotes will be more flavourful than large ones. They keep well in the fridge and can be stored for up to 1 month.

Main Uses and Cooking Tips

Chayotes have a fairly mild flavour and are best peeled and served simply in salads or salsas, with a squeeze of lime or orange juice and some chillies. If they are cooked, they should be seasoned well. The mild flavour makes them ideal for combining with other, more strongly flavoured ingredients. To cook *chayotes*, either peel and cook them in the same way as summer squash, or bake them.

Above: Winter squash

Baked Chayote

Cut them in half, brush the cut sides with oil, then either fill them with a vegetable stuffing or simply sprinkle them with salt, pepper and a little spice, if liked. Bake in a pre-heated oven at 190°C/375°F/Gas 5 for 25 minutes, or until tender all the way through when pierced with a skewer.

CHORIZO, DRIED MEAT AND SALT FISH

In hot countries dried and preserved foods are an important part of the diet. Mexico's traditional dried ingredients are very popular and are used to flavour many dishes.

CHORIZO

Chorizo is a highly seasoned pork sausage made from coarsely ground pork, garlic and spices. It is widely used in Mexican cookery in dishes as varied a apetizers, starters, soups, stews and casseroles. Mexican chorizo is made from fresh pork, unlike the Spanish chorizo, which is based upon smoked pork. The sausage mixture can be made up as needed and cooked immediately, just as it is, or packed into sausage skins. It can then be hung in a cool place and kept until required.

DRIED MEATS

Machaca is meat, usually beef, that has been salted and sun-dried before being shredded. This way of preparing meat is typical of northern Mexico, from Sonora in the west to Monterrey in the east. *Machaca* is often mixed with scrambled eggs, beans and cheese and wrapped in a flour tortilla. *Carne seca* (the term simply translates as "dried meat") is cut into chunks and served as an appetizer with fresh lime juice. It is one of the most popular dishes of the northern part of Mexico.

Below: Chorizo

Making Fresh Chorizo

As is so often the case, bought sausages can be good, but there is little comparison to the homemade product. Chorizo is easy to make, and you can prepare it in bulk, then freeze the surplus. Air-drying is best left to the experts.

MAKES ABOUT 900G/2LB

INGREDIENTS
    900g/2lb pork mince
    10ml/2 tsp each salt and ground
      black pepper
    2.5ml/½ tsp freshly grated nutmeg
    5ml/1 tsp dried thyme
    2.5ml/½ tsp ground anise
    2.5ml/½ tsp ground bay leaf
    3 garlic cloves, crushed
    120ml/4fl oz/½ cup sherry
      or brandy
    juice of 2 limes

1 Place the meat in a large bowl and mix in all the other ingredients. Cover and chill in the fridge for at least 4 hours or overnight, so that all the flavours blend together.

2 Fill sausage skins with the meat mixture to make individual sausages. Use the sausages immediately or freeze until required.

3 Cook by pricking the skins in several places, then immersing the sausages in a saucepan of boiling water. Continue to boil for 10 minutes or until the meat is thoroughly cooked.

4 If you prefer, you can shape the sausagemeat into small patties and fry these in a little fat, turning them once to ensure even cooking. Serve the sausages hot, with a spicy tomato-based sauce.

SALTED MEAT AND FISH

Salting was a useful way of preserving meat for long periods in the days before people had fridges. If a family slaughtered a pig or cow, every piece of the animal was utilized; by drying surplus meat or making it into sausages, it would have been possible to make it last for several months. Fish was salted for much the same reason, but what began as a necessity is now a delicacy as Mexicans became very fond of fish prepared in this manner. Today, when the need for preserving fish is not as pressing, salt fish, particularly cod, is still popular in Mexican, Spanish, Caribbean and even French cooking.

Soaking Salted Fish

To make it edible, salted fish should be soaked for several hours, preferably overnight. The fish will also have picked up grit and dirt, and is hard and stiff, and needs to be cleaned and softened before it is cooked. Place the fish in a large bowl of fresh water. Change the water frequently. After the fish has soaked for some time, test the water to see how salty it is. As it soaks the fish will become soft and pliable.

SALT COD

Buying and Storing

Salt cod is available from ethnic food stores and some supermarkets, and can be kept in a cupboard for several months before use. The pieces on display look incredibly unappetizing and are rock hard. They are also usually unwrapped and might have a slightly grimy appearance. Don't let this put you off, when it has been cleaned and rehydrated salt fish is perfectly safe to cook with and consume.

Main Uses and Cooking Tips

Before cooking, salt cod must be soaked in water for several hours, or overnight if possible. Change the water frequently to get rid of any dirt and to reduce the salt content. *Bacalao a la Vizcaìna* is a salt cod stew which originated in Spain, but is now the traditional dish for Christmas Eve dinner in Mexico. Salt cod can also be cooked and served with a chilli sauce or a classic fresh tomato or citrus salsa.

Right: Salt cod

Making *Machaca* at Home

This might seem an unusual technique for preparing beef, but the results make for a totally authentic experience of Mexican food.

INGREDIENTS
  900g/2lb sirloin steak, about
    5mm/¼in thick
  45ml/3 tbsp medium ground
    sea salt

1 Trim away any gristle from the meat and then sprinkle both sides with the sea salt.

2 Make a hole in each piece of meat and thread string through, or hang the meat from a butcher's hook.

3 Hang the meat for about 3 days in a cool dry place so it can dry out. Alternatively, place the meat on a raised grill pan or suspend it from a rotisserie bar, so that the air can circulate around it, and dry it out in an oven heated to the lowest setting.

4 When the meat is completely dry, place it in a bowl and pour over water to cover. Leave it to rehydrate for about 30 minutes.

5 Drain the meat, and shred it with two forks.

6 Spread it out to dry again. When it has dried, store it in a covered box in the fridge until required.

CHEESE

Being a complete protein, cheese was an important addition to the Mexican diet. Until its arrival, Mexicans' main sources of protein were beans and corn, both of which are incomplete. Cheese is widely used in Mexican cooking. The type for each dish is carefully chosen, and the properties – crumbling, melting, grating – are as important as the flavour.

In terms of the history of Mexican cuisine, cheese arrived on the scene fairly late. Before the Conquest in 1521, the main source of meat was the pig, and there was therefore no milk. The Spanish invaders established vast estates and introduced dairy cattle to the country. Milk, cream and butter were produced, and the monks who travelled with the conquerors taught the local people how to make cheeses. At first these were based on traditional Spanish cheeses such as Manchego, but the Mexicans soon developed several cheeses of their own. Today, the range includes cheeses made from goat's and ewe's milk, and also includes varieties that were introduced to Mexico by later immigrants.

There are many different cheeses available in Mexico, but there are a few types that deserve special mention. Unfortunately, Mexican cheeses are seldom sold outside

Below: Feta and ricotta can be used as substitutes for Mexican cheeses.

the country, so acceptable substitutes are suggested for cooks who are unable to access the authentic ingredient.

Below: Mozzarella can be used as a substitute for Asadero.

QUESO FRESCO

As the name suggests, *queso fresco* (fresh cheese) is young and unripened. *Queso fresco* is actually the generic name for a number of different cheeses, of all which share some common characteristics, being moist and creamy in colour, with a very mild flavour and a crumbly texture. The cheese is often used for crumbling over dishes such as scrambled eggs, cooked *nopales* (cactus leaves) or other vegetables. It is also used in tacos and other snacks based on tortillas.

Queso fresco has a clean, sharp taste and is a good melting cheese. If you can't locate it, substitute a good quality ricotta or mozzarella, preferably bought from a specialist Italian food store.

ASADERO

The name means "roasting cheese" and this is a mild curd cheese which is beautifully supple. *Asadero* is best when it is melted, and is ideal for stuffing chillies or other vegetables or meats, as it is unlikely to leak out. The closest equivalent is mozzarella.

Left: Queso Anejo

QUESO ANEJO

Anejo means "aged". This is a very mature, hard, dry cheese. Sharp and salty, it can be grated easily. *Anejo* is often used for sprinkling on the top of enchiladas. Parmesan cheese makes a good substitute.

QUESO CHIHUAHUA

This cheese resembles *anejo*, but is less salty. Substitute medium Cheddar cheese for it in recipes.

QUESO DE OAXACA

This is another stringy cheese that is ideal for cooking as it has good melting properties. It tastes slightly tart. Monterey Jack is recommended as a substitute in recipes.

Monterey Jack

Monterey Jack is a Californian cheese which originated as *queso del pais* ("country cheese"). Spanish missionaries taught the people of California to make it in the early part of the 18th century. The recipe, which is still being used today, was actually refined in Monterey, California, about 200 years ago. The "Jack" part of the name is reputed to owe its origin to David Jacks, who made the cheese in his dairy, the "s" being dropped when it was felt that the name Monterey Jack was more catchy.

The cheese has a mild flavour and creamy texture and is good to eat on its own as well as being a useful cooking cheese. It matures well, developing a sweet, nutty flavour as it ages. Monterey Jack can be substituted in any recipe calling for *Queso de Oaxaca*, *asadero* or *Chihuahua* cheese. Monterey Jack is very popular all over North America, and is now available in other countries too. If you can't locate Monterey Jack, a mild Cheddar cheese can be used.

Minguichi

Chillies and cheese make an excellent partnership, and the pairing is especially celebrated in dishes called *minguichi* in Michoacán and *chiles con queso* (chillies with cheese) in other areas. There are innumerable variations on the basic theme, using whatever ingredients are to hand. Serve *chiles con queso* on its own with corn tortillas or tortilla chips, or stir in some *Frijoles de Olla* to add more body to the dip. This dish is also very good if chipotle chillies (smoked jalapeños) are used instead of anchos.

In Mexico, this would be made with *crema*, a thick cream with a slightly acidic flavour. *Crema* is not readily available outside Mexico, so crème fraîche has been used instead.

MAKES ABOUT 750ML/1¼ PINTS/3 CUPS

INGREDIENTS
250ml/8fl oz/1 cup crème fraîche
225g/8oz/2 cups grated medium Cheddar cheese
2 ancho chillies, seeded and toasted until crisp

1 Spoon the crème fraîche into a heavy-based saucepan and cook over a low heat until warmed.

2 Add the cheese and stir until it melts. Crumble in the chillies and mix well, then pour into a bowl and serve immediately.

HERBS, SEASONINGS AND SPICES

Mexican cooking makes use of a wide range of flavourings. Chillies are clearly top of the list. There are so many different varieties that fresh and dried chillies, chilli powders and pastes can create a wide range of flavours, from fiery or merely spicy to supremely subtle. Chillies are by no means the only flavourings used in Mexico, however. Spices like cinnamon and allspice are popular and herbs also play an important role. Some, such as *epazote*, are native to the country, while others were first introduced by Spanish and other immigrant groups.

Achiote

This is the hard red-orange seed of the annatto tree, which is native to the warmer parts of South America, including some areas of Mexico. The seed is ground and added to food to give colour and flavour. Good quality, fresh achiote seeds give food a distinctive, earthy flavour. Achiote is used a lot in the Yucatán, where it is included in pastes that are spread on meats before cooking.

Allspice

This tree is native to Jamaica, although it may also have grown naturally in the coastal area of Mexico around Tabasco. Columbus is reputed to have brought it to Europe from Jamaica, having mistaken the berries for peppercorns – the Spanish call the spice *pimienta*, which means pepper. Allspice berries are picked, dried and ground or used whole. They are used in various types of *Escabeche* to add flavour to vegetables or fish which is being pickled, and are also added to meat dishes. They even feature in desserts and drinks.

Cinnamon

Sri Lankan cinnamon is used quite extensively in Mexican cookery in both sweet and savoury dishes. It was introduced during the colonial era, and is a favourite spice in chorizo sausages. It is also used in rice pudding and is added to drinks. Mexican chocolate, which is used to make hot drinks, contains cinnamon. Both ground cinnamon and sticks are used in Mexican cooking.

Cloves

Cloves were brought to Mexico from Asia, via Spain. They are used in the complex spice mixes that are so important in making *moles* and *pepiáns* for cooking with meat and poultry.

Coriander

Fresh coriander leaves, called cilantro in Mexico, are used in a number of savoury dishes and salsas. The herb is

Above: Allspice, top, cinnamon quills and ground cinnamon, and achiote, bottom.

Below: Cumin, right, coriander, left and cloves, bottom right.

Right: Oregano

Cumin Seeds

Cumin seeds are ground with other spices in some savoury dishes, but are neither used alone nor used in large quantities, as their taste would overpower other, more delicate flavours. Native to Egypt, cumin was introduced in Mexican cuisine during colonial times.

Tamarind

The dark brown, bean-shaped pod comes from the tamarind tree, which has grown in India for centuries. The Spanish introduced it to the West Indies in the 17th century, and it has been growing there ever since. Tamarind is usually marketed as a pressed block of pods and pulp – rather like a block of pressed stoned dates – and is often sold in Indian food shops. The taste is a refreshing mixture of sweet and sour.

Vanilla

Records depicting Aztec life reveal that they were familiar with vanilla, and there is also evidence that it was used

native to Europe, but is grown in South America too. It has a wonderful flavour and aroma. Coriander seeds are also used in some Mexican recipes, but the two should not be confused, nor should one be substituted for the other, as they have very different flavours.

Right: Vanilla

in Mexico in the 16th century as a flavouring for hot chocolate. Vanilla pods grow on vines, and until the 1800s, the spice was grown exclusively in Mexico. Good quality pods are very dark brown, waxy and malleable. The spice has a rich aroma and a sweet taste. It is perfect for adding to desserts and is also used to flavour drinks.

Epazote

This herb is widely used in Mexican cooking, but is, unfortunately, not available outside Mexico unless you grow it yourself. There is no real substitute for the distinctive, sharply pungent flavour of this fresh herb. *Epazote* is also useful because when it is cooked with beans such as black beans, it can help to relieve flatulence.

Oregano

There are several varieties of oregano grown in Mexico. The most popular type is from the verbena family; its flavour is stronger and more aromatic than that of the European varieties. Sold fresh or dried in markets across Mexico, oregano adds a delightful sweet note to *Escabeche*, stews and meat dishes.

Right: Tamarind

Vanilla Sugar

Place a vanilla pod in a large jar full of caster sugar. It gives the sugar a wonderful flavour, which is great in cakes, puddings and other sweet dishes, and one pod will flavour several jars full of sugar before it is exhausted.

ALCOHOLIC DRINKS

Mexico has a large number of fermented beverages, mainly derived from fruit or a plant called the agave. Many of these are an acquired taste and not particularly popular outside the country.

BEER

Mexicans were introduced to the brewing process by the German settlers who came to their country and many of the brewing companies in existence today have German roots. Mexican beer production centres largely around the north of the country, although there are breweries everywhere. The city of Monterrey in Nuevo León is renowned as the beer capital of Mexico. Many people are employed in brewing and subsidiary industries such as glass making, carton manufacture and label printing,

Above: Beers

and the beer industry is an important part of the economy. Mexican beer brands such as Dos Equis, Sol and Corona are exported, although these are often brewed outside Mexico on licence. Other brands, such as Tecate, which are less readily available, are worth trying.

WINE

Wine production on a large scale was actively discouraged during the years of Spanish rule as the conquerors wanted to promote wines and spirits from Spain. A wine industry finally did grow up, however, in Baja California, and even today, the major vineyards are in the north-west of the country, although there is some wine production further south. New World wines have become an important part of the wine market in recent years and there is increased interest in wines from Mexico, which are very reasonably priced. The popular grapes for the production of white wine are Chardonnay, Sauvignon Blanc,

Left: Red wine

Right: White wine

Riesling and Chenin Blanc, while established red grape varieties include Cabernet Sauvignon, Pinot Noir and Grenache, as well as Merlot.

PULQUE

Records from the time of Cortés make reference to *pulque* being drunk by the Aztecs. It is a beer-like drink made from the sap of the agave plant, which is commonly called *maguey* in Mexico. While chocolate drinks were the preserve of the ruling classes in 16th century Mexico, *pulque* was drunk by the common people. The drink is still popular today, and *pulquerìas*, small bars selling *pulque* are widespread. These bars were once reputed to be wild, dangerous places, and women, children and people in uniform were not allowed to frequent them.

The traditional method for making *pulque* has changed little since the days of the Aztecs. The sap is extracted from the plant, allowed to ferment for a few weeks, then drunk. If left, it would continue to ferment and would quite soon become undrinkable. The short life span of the product means that it is seldom sold outside Mexico.

Pulque, which is between 6 and 8 per cent proof, has a unique, slightly earthy flavour, and is very definitely an acquired taste. In Mexico, efforts to make it more universally acceptable include blending it with a fruit juice such as pineapple and selling it in cans.

Right: Pulque

KAHLÚA

This is a coffee liqueur made in Mexico city and popular throughout the world. It is added to fresh coffee to make after-dinner coffee and often features in cocktails. Kahlúa is delicious when drunk from a straight liqueur glass with a thin layer of cream floated on the top, and is also irresistible when blended with vanilla ice cream.

MESCAL

This is the generic name for agave spirit. Tequila, which will be discussed in more detail later, is just one type of *mescal*. Unfortunately, in western Europe, the name *mescal* is synonymous with one particular brand of the spirit, which has a *maguey* worm in the bottle. This has led to some monumental drinking

sessions as individuals competed to see who would be landed with the worm, and the reputation of *mescal* suffered in the process. For the record, the worm was originally placed in the bottle to demonstrate the alcoholic proof of the *mescal*, the argument being that the preservation of the worm (actually a moth larva) proved the potency of the alcohol. Oaxaca is largely credited by aficionados as being one of the best areas for *mescal* production. The traditional way of producing the spirit involves taking the heart or *piña* from a number of plants and cooking them in a large pit. An average *piña* will weigh about 50kg/110lb. The procedure begins with the digging of the pit. A large fire is built in the bottom and a layer of rocks is piled on top. When the fire has been burning under the rocks for about a day, the *piñas* are added. They are left to cook for 2–3 days. The cooking plays a large part in determining the flavour, aroma and smoothness of the *mescal*,

Left: Kahlúa

and is a skilled job. After cooking, the *piñas* are removed from the pit and crushed to release the juice. This, together with the fibrous part of the plant, is mixed with water and left to ferment. More modern methods, involving special ovens, are now used by commercial producers to cook the *piñas* and control the all-important fermentation process.

TEQUILA

Tequila is, without doubt, the Mexican spirit which is best known outside the country. A specific type of *mescal*, it is becoming steadily more popular, especially among younger drinkers.

The Spanish taught Mexicans the art of distilling. *Pulque*, the national drink made from the agave plant, was the perfect subject, and they began by distilling it to make *mescal*. This was then distilled a second time to produce tequila. If *mescal* is brandy, then tequila is Cognac, and is subject to similar

controls to those that are imposed by the French government on their famous spirit. There are also parallels with the production of Champagne, in that tequila production is tightly regulated and may only take place in specially designated areas.

Tequila takes its name from the eponymous town in Jalisco where it was first made. The name means "volcano" in the local Indian dialect. Jalisco is also the home of *mariachi* music, which possibly explains how tequila gained its image as a fun, party drink.

Production

Tequila is made from the sap of the blue agave plant, which is not a cactus, as is commonly believed, but is related to the amaryllis. The leaves of each plant are cut away to leave the *piña*,

which is then steam cooked. The juice is fermented, then distilled twice, the second time in a copper still, after which it is bottled or matured in casks. All aspects of the process are rigidly controlled and documented.

Flavour Variations

There are several different types of tequila, and innumerable brands of all of these. Each brand has a different flavour, determined by the soil and the climate where the agave was grown, the amount of sugar the agave contained and the finer details of the processing, including the cooking of the *piña* and the fermentation of the juice. Some tequilas are matured in casks, and the type of wood used, together with the duration of the ageing process, will also influence the flavour of the finished product.

Not all tequilas are 100 per cent agave spirit; some are blended with cane spirit, but by law tequila must contain at least 51 per cent agave spirit. Blended tequilas are becoming less popular in foreign markets as consumers become more discriminating. At one time

Left: Mescal

Right: Tequila

Left: Tequila blanco

Below: Tequila and lime

Right: A bottle of Tequila anejo

Types of Tequila

Joven or blanco tequila has been bottled immediately after distillation. It is usually clear, but can sometimes be golden in colour. This classification also includes tequilas that have been aged for less than 60 days.

Reposada tequila is golden in colour and has been aged in oak for 2–6 months. It has a more rounded flavour than joven tequila.

Anejo tequila has been aged in oak for a year or more and has a rich golden colour.

Curados is the name given to blanco or joven tequila that has been naturally flavoured. Cinnamon sticks, chillies, almonds and vanilla pods are among the whole flavourings used, but essences and syrups can also be used.

Developing a Taste for Tequila

The best way to become a discriminating tequila drinker is to try as many different brands and types as possible. Compare and contrast them in terms of their appearance, bouquet, viscosity and flavour. Few tequilas taste of only one thing; most are a complex blend of flavours. They may taste sweet, earthy, woody, smooth or even smoky. It is a good idea to taste a new tequila against a familiar brand to give a standard for comparison.

Tequila Drinking

Drinking a shot of tequila in the classic manner, with a lick of salt beforehand and a wedge of lime after, is one of the best ways for Europeans to sample this drink. The method was originally adopted because the spirit was so crude that salt and lime were deemed necessary to make it palatable.

A natural progression from the tequila shot was the margarita. The rim of the glass is dipped in salt, the lime juice and tequila are combined and

triple sec – orange liqueur – is added. A margarita may be served neat, as it comes out of the bottle, or over ice cubes, or "frozen" with crushed ice.

In Mexico, tequila is often sipped alternately with a glass of *sangrita*, a tomato juice flavoured with chillies and other seasonings. When the tequila and tomato juice are combined, the drink becomes a bloody maria.

Below: Two types of Curados; bottles of blanco tequila that have had flavouring added. Here a few red chillies have been added to the bottle on the left, and three vanilla pods to the one on the right. The tequila will take on the flavour of the chilli or vanilla in just a few days.

you could walk into a bar in Britain or Europe and find only one type of tequila – and that was primarily used for making margaritas. However, the increasing popularity of Mexican food has led to a gradual rise in the popularity of tequila and a greater appreciation of the various types, and in some places today there are even specialist tequila bars, which stock a vast range of different types and brands of this exciting spirit

Left: Margarita

THE RECIPES

Mexican cooking is so much more than enchiladas and empanadas, although these are both worthy of mention. Until relatively recently, many Mexican restaurants outside the country tended to serve Tex-Mex food, which owed its origins to Mexico, but had been modified by the country's northern neighbours. Today, discerning diners seek out places that serve true Mexican food — authentically colourful, imaginative and not necessarily fiery — and are keen to recreate their favourite dishes at home. Supermarkets, gourmet stores and mail-order suppliers have responded to the changing market by stocking specialist ingredients — even such unusual items as tomatillos and the less common varieties of chilli — and this has made it much easier for enthusiastic cooks to experiment with the diverse dishes that traditional Mexican cuisine offers. The recipes that follow are a cross section of the authentic regional dishes available in this exciting country, and hold the diversity of flavours, textures and methods that make classical Mexican cooking so fascinating and delicious.

SALSAS, SOUPS AND SNACKS

The bright colours, incomparable flavours and adaptability of salsas make them indispensable to any

good cook, and their usefulness extends far beyond the boundaries of Mexican cuisine. There are two

classifications of soup in Mexico: those that conform to the accepted definition, and consist of vegetables,

meat or fish cooked in a liquid, and those that come under the heading of sopa seca, *or "dry soup".*

Snacks cover a range of colourful little dishes that Mexicans nibble at throughout the day. Several of

these may be served together, rather like the Spanish tapas, to make an informal meal,

or they may appear as appetizers or starters

CLASSIC TOMATO SALSA

THIS IS THE TRADITIONAL TOMATO-BASED SALSA THAT MOST PEOPLE ASSOCIATE WITH MEXICAN FOOD. THERE ARE INNUMERABLE RECIPES FOR IT, BUT THE BASICS OF ONION, TOMATO, CHILLI AND CORIANDER ARE COMMON TO EVERY ONE OF THEM. SERVE THIS SALSA AS A CONDIMENT WITH A WIDE VARIETY OF DISHES.

SERVES SIX AS AN ACCOMPANIMENT

INGREDIENTS

   3–6 fresh serrano chillies
   1 large white onion
   grated rind and juice of 2 limes, plus
     strips of lime rind, to garnish
   8 ripe, firm tomatoes
   large bunch of fresh coriander
   1.5ml/¼ tsp caster sugar
   salt

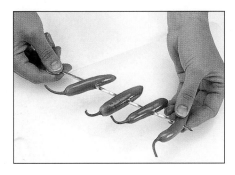

1 Use three chillies for a salsa of medium heat; up to six if you like it hot. To peel the chillies spear them on a long-handled metal skewer and roast them over the flame of a gas burner until the skins blister and darken. Do not let the flesh burn. Alternatively, dry fry them in a griddle pan until the skins are scorched.

2 Place the roasted chillies in a strong plastic bag and tie the top of the bag to keep the steam in. Set aside for about 20 minutes.

3 Meanwhile, chop the onion finely and put it in a bowl with the lime rind and juice. The lime juice will soften the onion.

VARIATIONS
Use spring onions or mild red onions instead of white onion. For a smoky flavour, use chipotle chillies instead of fresh serrano chillies.

4 Remove the chillies from the bag and peel off the skins. Cut off the stalks, then slit the chillies and scrape out the seeds with a sharp knife. Chop the flesh roughly and set aside.

5 Cut a small cross in the base of each tomato. Place the tomatoes in a heatproof bowl and pour over boiling water to cover.

6 Leave the tomatoes in the water for 3 minutes, then lift them out using a slotted spoon and plunge them into a bowl of cold water. Drain. The skins will have begun to peel back from the crosses. Remove the skins completely.

7 Dice the peeled tomatoes and put them in a bowl. Add the chopped onion which should have softened, together with the lime mixture. Chop the fresh coriander finely.

8 Add the coriander to the salsa, with the chillies and the sugar. Mix gently until the sugar has dissolved and all the ingredients are coated in lime juice. Cover and chill for 2–3 hours to allow the flavours to blend. The salsa will keep for 3–4 days in the fridge. Garnish with the strips of lime rind just before serving.

FRIJOLES DE OLLA

Travellers often say that "beans in a pot", as it is translated, taste different in Mexico from those cooked anywhere else. The secret is, quite literally, in the pot. Traditionally, clay pots are used, which give the beans a wonderful, slightly earthy flavour. This dish would be served as just one of the courses in a formal Mexican meal.

SERVES FOUR

INGREDIENTS
  250g/9oz/1¼ cups dried pinto beans,
    soaked overnight in water to cover
  1.75 litres/3 pints/7½ cups water
  2 onions
  10 garlic cloves, peeled and
    left whole
  small bunch of fresh coriander
  salt
For the toppings
  2 fresh red fresno chillies
  1 tomato, peeled and chopped
  2 spring onions, finely chopped
  60ml/4 tbsp soured cream
  50g/2oz feta cheese

COOK'S TIP
In Mexico, the local fresh cheese – *queso fresco* – would be used as the topping, but feta makes an acceptable substitute.

1 Drain the beans, rinse them under cold water and drain again. Put the water in a large saucepan, bring to the boil and add the beans.

2 Cut the onions in half and add them to the pan, with the whole garlic cloves. Bring to the boil again, then lower the heat and simmer for 1½ hours, until the beans are tender and there is only a little liquid remaining.

3 While the beans are cooking, prepare the toppings. Spear the chillies on a long-handled metal skewer and roast them over the flame of a gas burner until the skins blister and darken. Do not let the flesh burn. Alternatively, dry fry them in a griddle pan until the skins are scorched. Put the roasted chillies in a strong plastic bag and tie the top immediately to keep the steam in. Set aside for 20 minutes.

4 Remove the chillies from the bag and peel off the skins. Cut off the stalks, then slit the chillies and scrape out the seeds. Cut the flesh into thin strips and put it in a bowl. Spoon all the other toppings into separate bowls.

5 Ladle about 250ml/8fl oz/1 cup of the beans and liquid into a food processor or blender. Process to a smooth purée. If you prefer, simply mash the beans with a potato masher.

6 Return the bean purée to the pan, and stir it in. Chop the coriander, reserving some leaves to garnish, season with salt and mix well. Ladle the beans into warmed individual bowls and take them to the table with the toppings.

7 Serve the beans with the toppings and add coriander to garnish. Traditionally, each guest spoons a little of the chillies, tomatoes and spring onions over the beans, then adds a spoonful of soured cream. The finishing touch is a little feta cheese, crumbled over each portion.

GUACAMOLE

ONE OF THE BEST LOVED MEXICAN SALSAS, THIS BLEND OF CREAMY AVOCADO, TOMATOES, CHILLIES, CORIANDER AND LIME NOW APPEARS ON TABLES THE WORLD OVER. BOUGHT GUACAMOLE USUALLY CONTAINS MAYONNAISE, WHICH HELPS TO PRESERVE THE AVOCADO, BUT THIS IS NOT AN INGREDIENT IN TRADITIONAL RECIPES.

SERVES SIX TO EIGHT

INGREDIENTS
    4 medium tomatoes
    4 ripe avocados, preferably fuerte
    juice of 1 lime
    ½ small onion
    2 garlic cloves
    small bunch of fresh coriander,
      chopped
    3 fresh red fresno chillies
    salt
    tortilla chips, to serve

1 Cut a cross in the base of each tomato. Place the tomatoes in a heatproof bowl and pour over boiling water to cover.

2 Leave the tomatoes in the water for 3 minutes, then lift them out using a slotted spoon and plunge them into a bowl of cold water. Drain. The skins will have begun to peel back from the crosses. Remove the skins completely. Cut the tomatoes in half, remove the seeds with a teaspoon, then chop the flesh roughly and set it aside.

COOK'S TIP
Smooth-skinned fuerte avocados are native to Mexico, so would be ideal for this dip. If they are not available, use any avocados, but make sure they are ripe. To test, gently press the top of the avocado; it should give a little.

3 Cut the avocados in half then remove the stones. Scoop the flesh out of the shells and place it in a food processor or blender. Process until almost smooth, then scrape into a bowl and stir in the lime juice.

4 Chop the onion finely, then crush the garlic. Add both to the avocado and mix well. Stir in the coriander.

5 Remove the stalks from the chillies, slit them and scrape out the seeds with a small sharp knife. Chop the chillies finely and add them to the avocado mixture, with the chopped tomatoes. Mix well.

6 Check the seasoning and add salt to taste. Cover closely with clear film or a tight-fitting lid and chill for 1 hour before serving as a dip with tortilla chips. If it is well covered, guacamole will keep in the fridge for 2–3 days.

REFRIED BEANS

THESE ARE NOT ACTUALLY FRIED TWICE, BUT THEY ARE COOKED TWICE, FIRST AS FRIJOLES DE OLLA AND THEN BY FRYING IN LARD. IF THE ONLY REFRIED BEANS YOU'VE TRIED HAVE BEEN THE CANNED ONES, YOU MAY HAVE FOUND THEM RATHER BLAND. THESE, HOWEVER, ARE SUPERB.

SERVES FOUR

INGREDIENTS
  25g/1oz/2 tbsp lard
  2 onions, finely chopped
  5ml/1 tsp ground cumin
  5ml/1 tsp ground coriander
  1 quantity *Frijoles de Olla*, without
    the toppings
  3 garlic cloves, crushed
  small bunch of fresh coriander or
    4–5 dried avocado leaves
  50g/2oz feta cheese
  salt

1 Melt the lard in a large frying pan. Add the onions, cumin and ground coriander. Cook gently over a low heat for about 30 minutes or until the onions caramelize and become soft.

2 Add a ladleful of the soft, cooked beans. Fry them for only a few minutes simply to heat. Mash the beans into the onions as they cook, using a fork or a potato masher. Continue until all the beans have been added, a little at a time, then stir in the crushed garlic.

3 Lower the heat and cook the beans to form a thick paste. Season with salt and spoon into a warmed serving dish. Chop the coriander or crumble the avocado leaves, and sprinkle most of them over the beans. Crumble the feta cheese over the top, then garnish with the reserved sprigs or leaves.

JICAMA, CHILLI <u>AND</u> LIME SALAD

A VERY TASTY, CRISP VEGETABLE, THE JICAMA IS SOMETIMES CALLED THE MEXICAN POTATO. UNLIKE POTATO, HOWEVER, IT CAN BE EATEN RAW AS WELL AS COOKED. THIS MAKES A GOOD SALAD OR AN APPETIZER TO SERVE WITH DRINKS.

SERVES FOUR

INGREDIENTS
1 *jicama*
2.5ml/½ tsp salt
2 fresh serrano chillies
2 limes

1 Peel the *jicama* with a potato peeler or knife, then cut it into 2cm/¾in cubes. Put these in a large bowl, add the salt and toss well.

2 Cut the chillies in half, scrape out the seeds with a sharp knife, then cut the flesh into fine strips. Grate one of the limes thinly, removing only the coloured part of the skin, then cut the lime in half and squeeze the juice.

3 Add the chillies, lime rind and juice to the *jicama* and mix thoroughly to ensure that all the *jicama* cubes are coated. Cut the other lime into wedges.

4 Cover and chill for at least 1 hour before serving with lime wedges. If the salad is to be served as an appetizer with drinks, transfer the *jicama* cubes to little bowls and offer them with cocktail sticks for spearing.

COOK'S TIP
Look for *jicama* in Oriental supermarkets, as it is widely used in Chinese cooking. It goes by several names and you may find it labelled as either yam bean or Chinese turnip.

TLALPEÑO-STYLE SOUP

This simple chicken soup originates from Tlalpan, a suburb of Mexico City. The soup is made more substantial by the addition of cheese and chick-peas.

SERVES SIX

INGREDIENTS
1.5 litres/2½ pints/6¼ cups
 chicken stock
½ chipotle chilli, seeded
2 skinless, boneless chicken breasts
1 medium avocado
4 spring onions, finely sliced
400g/14oz can chick-peas, drained
salt and ground black pepper
75g/3oz/¾ cup grated Cheddar
 cheese, to serve

1 Pour the stock into a large saucepan and add the dried chilli. Bring to the boil, add the whole chicken breasts, then lower the heat and simmer for about 10 minutes or until the chicken is cooked. Remove the chicken from the pan and let it cool a little.

2 Using two forks, shred the chicken into small pieces. Set it aside. Pour the stock and chilli into a blender or food processor and process until smooth. Return the stock to the pan.

COOK'S TIP
When buying the avocado for this soup choose one that is slightly under-ripe, which makes it easier to handle when peeling and slicing.

3 Cut the avocado in half, remove the skin and seed, then slice the flesh into 2cm/¾in pieces. Add it to the stock, with the spring onions and chick-peas. Return the shredded chicken to the pan, with salt and pepper to taste, and heat gently.

4 Spoon the soup into heated bowls. Sprinkle grated cheese on top of each portion and serve immediately.

CORN SOUP

Quick and easy to prepare, this colourful soup has a sweet and creamy flavour. Children love it.

SERVES SIX

INGREDIENTS
2 red peppers
30ml/2 tbsp vegetable oil
1 medium onion, finely chopped
500g/1¼lb/3–4 cups sweetcorn
 niblets, thawed if frozen
750ml/1¼ pints/3 cups chicken stock
150ml/¼ pint/⅔ cup single cream
salt and ground black pepper

1 Dry fry the peppers in a griddle pan over a moderate heat, turning them frequently until the skins are blistered all over. Place them in a strong plastic bag and tie the top to keep the steam in. Set aside for 20 minutes, then remove the peppers from the bag and peel off the skin.

2 Cut the peppers in half and scoop out the seeds and cores. Set one aside. Cut the other into 1cm/½in dice.

3 Heat the oil in a large saucepan. Add the onion and fry over a low heat for about 10 minutes, until it is translucent and soft. Stir in the diced pepper and sweetcorn and fry for 5 minutes over a moderate heat.

4 Spoon the contents of the pan into a food processor, pour in the chicken stock and process until almost smooth. This processing can be done in batches if necessary.

5 Return the soup to the pan and reheat it. Stir in the cream, with salt and pepper to taste. Core, seed and cut the reserved pepper into thin strips and add half of these to the pan. Serve the soup in heated bowls, garnished with the remaining pepper strips.

COOK'S TIP
Look out for roasted red peppers in jars. These come ready-skinned and are useful in all sorts of recipes. Used here, they make a quick soup even speedier.

TORTILLA SOUP

THERE ARE SEVERAL TORTILLA SOUPS. THIS ONE IS AN AGUADA — OR LIQUID — VERSION, AND IS INTENDED FOR SERVING AS A STARTER OR LIGHT MEAL. IT IS VERY EASY AND QUICK TO PREPARE, OR MAKE IT IN ADVANCE AND FRY THE TORTILLA MEZES AS IT REHEATS. THE CRISP TORTILLA PIECES ADD AN UNUSUAL TEXTURE.

SERVES FOUR

INGREDIENTS
    4 corn tortillas, freshly made or a few
      days old
    15ml/1 tbsp vegetable oil, plus extra,
      for frying
    1 small onion, finely chopped
    2 garlic cloves, crushed
    400g/14oz can plum tomatoes, drained
    1 litre/1¾ pints/4 cups chicken stock
    small bunch of fresh coriander
    salt and ground black pepper

1 Using a sharp knife, cut each tortilla into four or five strips, each measuring about 2cm/¾in wide.

2 Pour vegetable oil to a depth of 2cm/¾in into a heavy-based frying pan. Heat until a small piece of tortilla, added to the oil, floats on the top and bubbles at the edges.

3 Add a few tortilla strips to the hot oil and fry for a few minutes until crisp and golden brown all over, turning them occasionally. Remove with a slotted spoon and drain on a double layer of kitchen paper. Cook the remaining tortilla strips in the same way.

4 Heat the 15ml/1 tbsp vegetable oil in a large heavy-based saucepan. Add the chopped onion and garlic and cook over a moderate heat for 2–3 minutes, stirring constantly with a wooden spatula, until the onion is soft and translucent. Do not let the garlic turn brown or it will give the soup a bitter taste.

5 Chop the tomatoes using a large sharp knife and add them to the onion mixture in the pan. Pour in the chicken stock and stir well. Bring to the boil, then lower the heat and allow to simmer for about 10 minutes, until the liquid has reduced slightly.

6 Chop the coriander. Add to the soup, reserving a little to use as a garnish. Season to taste.

7 Place a few of the crisp tortilla pieces in the bottom of four warmed soup bowls. Ladle the soup on top. Sprinkle each portion with the reserved chopped coriander and serve.

COOK'S TIP
An easy way to chop the coriander is to put the coriander leaves in a mug and snip with a pair of scissors. Hold the scissors vertically in both hands and work the blades back and forth until the coriander is finely chopped.

CHILLIES RELLENOS

STUFFED CHILLIES ARE POPULAR ALL OVER MEXICO. THE TYPE OF CHILLI USED DIFFERS FROM REGION TO REGION, BUT LARGER CHILLIES ARE OBVIOUSLY EASIER TO STUFF THAN SMALLER ONES. POBLANOS AND ANAHEIMS ARE QUITE MILD, BUT YOU CAN USE HOTTER CHILLIES IF YOU PREFER.

MAKES SIX

INGREDIENTS
   6 fresh poblano or Anaheim chillies
   2 potatoes, total weight about
      400g/14oz
   200g/7oz/scant 1 cup cream cheese
   200g/7oz/1¾ cups grated mature
      Cheddar cheese
   5ml/1 tsp salt
   2.5ml/½ tsp ground black pepper
   2 eggs, separated
   115g/4oz/1 cup plain flour
   2.5ml/½ tsp white pepper
   oil, for frying
   chilli flakes to garnish, optional

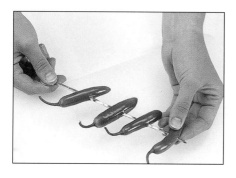

1 Make a neat slit down one side of each chilli. Place them in a dry frying pan over a moderate heat, turning them frequently until the skins blister.

2 Place the chillies in a strong plastic bag and tie the top to keep the steam in. Set aside for 20 minutes, then carefully peel off the skins and remove the seeds through the slits, keeping the chillies whole. Dry the chillies with kitchen paper and set them aside.

COOK'S TIP
Take care when making the filling; mix gently, trying not to break up the potato pieces.

VARIATION
Whole ancho (dried poblano) chillies can be used instead of fresh chillies, but will need to be reconstituted in water before they can be seeded and stuffed.

3 Scrub or peel the potatoes and cut them into 1cm/½in dice. Bring a large saucepan of water to the boil, add the potatoes and let the water return to boiling point. Lower the heat and simmer for 5 minutes or until the potatoes are just tender. Do not overcook. Drain them thoroughly.

4 Put the cream cheese in a bowl and stir in the grated cheese, with 2.5ml/ ½ tsp of the salt and the black pepper. Add the potato and mix gently.

5 Spoon some of the potato filling into each chilli. Put them on a plate, cover with clear film and chill for 1 hour so that the filling becomes firm.

6 Put the egg whites in a clean, grease-free bowl and whisk them to firm peaks. In a separate bowl, beat the yolks until pale, then fold in the whites. Scrape the mixture on to a large, shallow dish. Spread out the flour in another shallow dish and season it with the remaining salt and the white pepper.

7 Heat the oil for deep frying to 190°C/ 375°F. Coat a few chillies first in flour and then in egg before adding carefully to the hot oil.

8 Fry the chillies in batches until golden and crisp. Drain on kitchen paper and serve hot, garnished with a sprinkle of chilli flakes for extra heat, if desired.

EMPANADAS WITH ROPAS VIEJAS

THE FILLING FOR THESE EMPANADAS IS TRADITIONALLY MADE WITH MEAT THAT IS COOKED UNTIL IT IS SO TENDER THAT IT CAN BE TORN APART WITH FORKS. IT RESEMBLES TATTERED CLOTH, WHICH IS HOW IT CAME TO BE KNOWN AS ROPA VIEJA, WHICH MEANS "OLD CLOTHES".

SERVES SIX (TWELVE EMPANADAS)

INGREDIENTS

150g/5oz/1 cup *masa harina*
30ml/2 tbsp plain flour
2.5ml/½ tsp salt
120–150ml/4–5fl oz/½–⅔ cup
  warm water
15ml/1 tbsp oil, plus extra, for frying
250g/9oz lean minced pork
1 garlic clove, crushed
3 tomatoes
2 ancho chillies
½ small onion
2.5ml/½ tsp ground cumin
2.5ml/½ tsp salt

1 Mix the *masa harina*, plain flour and salt in a bowl. Gradually add enough of the warm water to make a smooth, but not sticky, dough. Knead briefly, then shape into a ball, wrap in clear film and set aside.

2 Heat 15ml/1 tbsp oil in a saucepan. Add the minced pork and cook, stirring frequently, until it has browned evenly. Stir in the garlic and cook for 2 minutes more. Remove from the heat and set the pan aside.

3 Cut a cross in the base of each tomato, place them in a bowl and pour over boiling water. After 3 minutes plunge the tomatoes into a bowl of cold water. Drain. The skins will peel back easily from the crosses. Remove the skins completely. Chop the tomato flesh and put in a bowl.

4 Slit the ancho chillies and scrape out the seeds. Chop the chillies finely and add them to the tomatoes. Chop the onion finely and add it to the tomato mixture, with the ground cumin.

5 Stir the tomato mixture into the pan containing the pork and cook over a moderate heat for 10 minutes, stirring occasionally. Season with salt to taste.

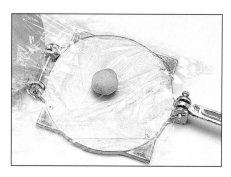

6 To make the tortillas, divide the empanada dough into 12 pieces and roll each piece into a ball. Open a tortilla press and line both sides with plastic (this can be cut from a new plastic sandwich bag). Put a ball of dough on the press and bring the top down to flatten it into a 7.5cm/3in round. Use the remaining dough balls to make more tortillas in the same way.

COOK'S TIP
If the empanada dough proves difficult to handle, a little oil or melted lard can be kneaded into the dough to help make it more pliable.

7 Spoon a little of the meat mixture on one half of each tortilla, working quickly to stop the dough from drying out. Dampen the edges of the dough with a little water and fold, turnover-style, to make the empanadas.

8 Seal the edges on the empanadas by pinching them between the index finger and thumb of the left hand and the index finger of the right hand.

9 Heat a little oil in a large frying pan. When it is hot, fry the empanadas in batches until crisp and golden on both sides, turning at least once. Serve hot or cold.

TORTAS

The multi-layered filling of Tortas offers lots of different tastes and textures. Traditionally they are made using rolls called TELERAS.

SERVES TWO

INGREDIENTS

2 fresh jalapeño chillies
juice of ½ lime
2 French bread rolls or 2 pieces
   of French bread
115g/4oz/⅔ cup Refried Beans
150g/5oz roast pork
2 small tomatoes, sliced
115g/4oz Cheddar cheese, sliced
small bunch of fresh coriander
30ml/2 tbsp crème fraîche

VARIATIONS

The essential ingredients of a *torta* are refried beans and chillies. Everything else is subject to change. Ham, chicken or turkey could all be used instead of pork, and lettuce is often added.

1 Cut the chillies in half, scrape out the seeds, then cut the flesh into thin strips. Put it in a bowl, pour over the lime juice and leave to stand.

2 If using rolls, slice them in half and remove some of the crumb so that they are slightly hollowed. If using French bread, slice each piece in half lengthways. Set the top of each piece of bread or roll aside and spread the bottom halves with the refried beans.

3 Cut the pork into thin shreds and put these on top of the refried beans. Top with the tomato slices. Drain the jalapeño strips and put them on top of the tomato slices. Add the cheese and sprinkle with coriander leaves.

4 Turn the top halves of the bread or rolls over, so that the cut sides are uppermost, and spread these with crème fraîche. Sandwich back together again and serve.

TAQUITOS WITH BEEF

MINIATURE *SOFT CORN TORTILLAS MOULDED AROUND A TASTY FILLING AND SERVED WARM. UNLESS YOU HAVE ACCESS TO MINIATURE FRESH CORN TORTILLAS, YOU WILL NEED A TORTILLA PRESS.*

2 Mix the *masa harina* and salt in a large bowl. Add the warm water, a little at a time, to make a dough that can be worked into a ball. Knead this on a lightly floured surface for 3–4 minutes until smooth, then wrap the dough in clear film and leave to rest for 1 hour.

3 Divide the dough into 12 small balls. Open a tortilla press and line both sides with plastic (this can be cut from a new plastic sandwich bag). Put a ball on the press and bring the top down to flatten it into a 5–6cm/2–2½in round. Flatten the remaining dough balls in the same way to make more tortillas.

4 Heat a griddle or frying pan until hot. Cook each tortilla for 15–20 seconds on each side, and then for a further 15 minutes on the first side. Keep the tortillas warm and soft by folding them inside a slightly damp dish towel.

5 Add the oregano, cumin, tomato purée and caster sugar to the pan containing the reserved beef cubes, with a couple of tablespoons of the reserved beef stock, or just enough to keep the mixture moist. Cook gently for a few minutes to combine the flavour.

6 Place a little of the lettuce on a warm tortilla. Top with a little of the filling and a little onion relish, fold in half and serve while still warm. Fill more tortillas in the same way.

SERVES TWELVE

INGREDIENTS
  500g/1¼lb rump steak, diced into
    1cm/½in pieces
  2 garlic cloves, peeled and left whole
  750ml/1¼ pints/3 cups beef stock
  150g/5oz/1 cup *masa harina*
  pinch of salt
  120ml/4fl oz/½ cup warm water
  7.5ml/1½ tsp dried oregano
  2.5ml/½ tsp ground cumin
  30ml/2 tbsp tomato purée
  2.5ml/½ tsp caster sugar
  salt and ground black pepper
  shredded lettuce to serve

1 Put the beef and whole garlic cloves in a large saucepan and cover with the beef stock. Bring to the boil, lower the heat and simmer for 10–15 minutes, until the meat is tender. Using a slotted spoon, transfer the meat to a clean pan and set it aside. Reserve the stock.

QUESADILLAS

THESE CHEESE-FILLED TORTILLAS ARE THE MEXICAN EQUIVALENT OF TOASTED SANDWICHES. SERVE THEM AS SOON AS THEY ARE COOKED, OR THEY WILL BECOME CHEWY. IF YOU ARE MAKING THEM FOR A CROWD, FILL AND FOLD THE TORTILLAS AHEAD OF TIME, BUT ONLY COOK THEM TO ORDER.

SERVES FOUR

INGREDIENTS

200g/7oz mozzarella, Monterey Jack
  or mild Cheddar cheese
1 fresh fresno chilli (optional)
8 wheat flour tortillas, about
  15cm/6in across
Classic Tomato Salsa to serve

VARIATIONS

Try spreading a thin layer of your favourite Mexican salsa on the tortilla before adding the cheese, or adding a few pieces of cooked chicken or prawns before folding the tortilla in half.

1 If using mozzarella cheese, it must be drained thoroughly and then patted dry and sliced into thin strips. Monterey Jack and Cheddar cheese should both be coarsely grated, as finely grated cheese will melt and ooze away when cooking. Set the cheese aside in a bowl.

2 If using the chilli, spear it on a long-handled metal skewer and roast it over the flame of a gas burner until the skin blisters and darkens. Do not let the flesh burn. Alternatively, dry fry it in a griddle pan until the skin is scorched. Place the roasted chilli in a strong plastic bag and tie the top to keep the steam in. Set aside for 20 minutes.

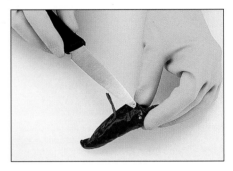

3 Remove the chilli from the bag and peel off the skin. Cut off the stalk, then slit the chilli and scrape out the seeds. Cut the flesh into eight thin strips.

4 Warm a large frying pan or griddle. Place one tortilla on the pan or griddle at a time, sprinkle about an eighth of the cheese on to one half and add a strip of chilli, if using. Fold the tortilla over the cheese and press the edges together gently to seal. Cook the filled tortilla for 1 minute, then turn over and cook the other side for 1 minute.

5 Remove the filled tortilla from the pan or griddle, cut it into three triangles or four strips and serve at once, with the tomato salsa

MEXICAN RICE

VERSIONS OF THIS DISH — A RELATIVE OF SPANISH RICE — ARE POPULAR ALL OVER SOUTH AMERICA. CLASSIFIED AS A SOPA SECA OR DRY SOUP, IT IS A DELICIOUS MEDLEY OF RICE, TOMATOES AND AROMATIC FLAVOURINGS. THE STOCK IN WHICH THE RICE IS COOKED IS LARGELY ABSORBED BY THE TIME THE DISH IS READY TO BE SERVED.

SERVES SIX

INGREDIENTS
  200g/7oz/1 cup long grain rice
  200g/7oz can chopped tomatoes in
    tomato juice
  ½ onion, roughly chopped
  2 garlic cloves, roughly chopped
  30ml/2 tbsp vegetable oil
  450ml/¾ pint/scant 2 cups chicken
    stock
  2.5ml/½ tsp salt
  3 fresh fresno chillies or other fresh
    green chillies, trimmed
  150g/5oz/1 cup frozen peas (optional)
  ground black pepper

1 Put the rice in a large heatproof bowl and pour over boiling water to cover. Stir once, then leave to stand for 10 minutes. Tip into a strainer over the sink, rinse under cold water, then drain again. Set aside to dry slightly.

2 Meanwhile, pour the tomatoes and juice into a food processor or blender, add the onion and garlic and process until smooth.

3 Heat the oil in a large, heavy-based pan, add the rice and cook over a moderate heat until it becomes a delicate golden brown. Stir occasionally to ensure that the rice does not stick to the bottom of the pan.

4 Add the tomato mixture and stir over a moderate heat until all the liquid has been absorbed. Stir in the stock, salt, whole chillies and peas, if using. Continue to cook the mixture, stirring occasionally, until all the liquid has been absorbed and the rice is just tender.

5 Remove the pan from the heat, cover it with a tight-fitting lid and leave it to stand in a warm place for 5–10 minutes. Remove the chillies, fluff up the rice lightly and serve, sprinkled with black pepper. The chillies may be used as a garnish, if liked.

COOK'S TIP
Do not stir the rice too often after adding the stock or the grains will break down and the mixture will become starchy.

TORTILLA CHIPS

THESE ARE KNOWN AS TOTOPOS IN MEXICO, AND THE TERM REFERS TO BOTH THE FRIED TORTILLA STRIPS USED TO GARNISH SOUPS AND THE TRIANGLES OF CORN TORTILLA USED FOR SCOOPING SALSA OR DIPS. USE TORTILLAS THAT ARE A FEW DAYS OLD; FRESH ONES WILL NOT CRISP UP SO WELL.

SERVES FOUR

INGREDIENTS
  4–8 corn tortillas
  oil, for frying
  salt

VARIATION
When fried, wheat flour tortillas do not crisp up as well as corn tortillas, but they make a delicious sweet treat when sprinkled with ground cinnamon and caster sugar. Serve them hot with cream.

1 Cut each tortilla into six triangular wedges. Pour oil into a large frying pan to a depth of 1cm/½in, place the pan over a moderate heat and heat until very hot (see Cook's Tip).

COOK'S TIP
The oil needs to be very hot for cooking the tortillas – test it by carefully adding one of the wedges. It should float and begin to bubble in the oil immediately.

2 Fry the tortilla wedges in the hot oil in small batches until they turn golden and are crisp. This will only take a few moments. Remove with a slotted spoon and drain on kitchen paper. Sprinkle with salt.

3 *Totopos* should be served warm. They can be cooled completely and stored in an airtight container for a few days, but will need to be reheated in a microwave or a warm oven before being served.

PEPITAS

THESE LITTLE SNACKS ARE ABSOLUTELY IRRESISTIBLE, ESPECIALLY IF YOU INCLUDE CHIPOTLE CHILLIES. THEIR SMOKY FLAVOUR IS THE PERFECT FOIL FOR THE NUTTY TASTE OF THE PUMPKIN SEEDS AND THE SWEETNESS CONTRIBUTED BY THE SUGAR. SERVE THEM WITH PRE-DINNER DRINKS.

SERVES FOUR

INGREDIENTS
  130g/4½oz/1 cup pumpkin seeds
  4 garlic cloves, crushed
  1.5ml/¼ tsp salt
  10ml/2 tsp crushed dried chillies
  5ml/1 tsp caster sugar
  a wedge of lime

COOK'S TIP
It is important to keep the pumpkin seeds moving as they cook. Watch them carefully and do not let them burn, or they will taste bitter.

1 Heat a small heavy-based frying pan, add the pumpkin seeds and dry fry for a few minutes, stirring constantly as they swell.

2 When all the seeds have swollen, add the garlic and cook for a few minutes more, stirring all the time. Add the salt and the crushed chillies and stir to mix. Turn off the heat, but keep the pan on the stove. Sprinkle sugar over the seeds and shake the pan to ensure that they are all coated.

3 Tip the *pepitas* into a bowl and serve with the wedge of lime for squeezing over the seeds. If the lime is omitted, the seeds can be cooled and stored in an airtight container for reheating later, but they are best served fresh.

MAIN
DISHES

 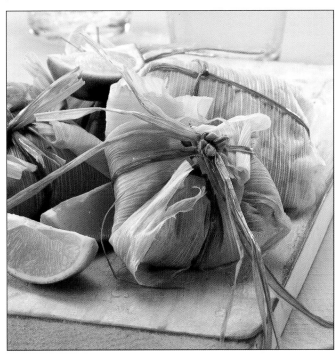

The main part of a Mexican meal is the meat or fish course, and the variety of ingredients that are used reflect

the range of Mexico's produce. This chapter includes favourite Mexican meat and fish dishes,

from Chicken Fajitas and Tacos with Shredded Beef to Stuffed Loin of Pork and the classic Turkey Mole.

It also features fish dishes such as the Spanish influenced Escabeche, and the family

favourite Salt Cod for Christmas Eve.

BURRITOS WITH CHICKEN AND RICE

IN MEXICO, BURRITOS ARE A POPULAR STREET FOOD, EATEN ON THE HOOF. THE SECRET OF A SUCCESSFUL BURRITO IS TO HAVE ALL THE FILLING NEATLY PACKAGED INSIDE THE TORTILLA FOR EASY EATING, SO THESE SNACKS ARE SELDOM SERVED WITH A POUR-OVER SAUCE.

SERVES FOUR

INGREDIENTS
   90g/3½oz/½ cup long grain rice
   15ml/1 tbsp vegetable oil
   1 onion, chopped
   2.5ml/½ tsp ground cloves
   5ml/1 tsp dried, or fresh oregano
   200g/7oz can chopped tomatoes in
      tomato juice
   2 skinless, boneless chicken breasts
   150g/5oz/1¼ cups grated Monterey
      Jack or mild Cheddar cheese
   60ml/4 tbsp soured cream (optional)
   8 x 20–25cm/8–10in fresh wheat
      flour tortillas
   salt
   fresh oregano, to garnish (optional)

1 Bring a saucepan of lightly salted water to the boil. Add the rice and cook for 8 minutes. Drain, rinse and then drain again.

2 Heat the oil in a large saucepan. Add the onion, with the ground cloves and oregano, and fry for 2–3 minutes. Stir in the rice and tomatoes and cook over a low heat until all the tomato juice has been absorbed. Set the pan aside.

3 Put the chicken breasts in a large saucepan, pour in enough water to cover and bring to the boil. Lower the heat and simmer for about 10 minutes or until the chicken is cooked through. Lift the chicken out of the pan, put on a plate and cool slightly.

4 Preheat the oven to 160°C/325°F/ Gas 3. Shred the chicken by pulling the flesh apart with two forks, then add the chicken to the rice mixture, with the grated cheese. Stir in the soured cream, if using.

COOK'S TIP
If you use very fresh tortillas, you may be able to dispense with the cocktail sticks. Secure the tortilla parcels by damping the final fold with a little water. When you lay the burritos in the dish, place them with the folded surfaces down.

5 Wrap the tortillas in foil and place them on a plate. Stand the plate over boiling water for about 5 minutes. Alternatively, wrap in microwave-safe film and heat in a microwave on full power for 1 minute.

6 Spoon one-eighth of the filling into the centre of a tortilla and fold in both sides. Fold the bottom up and the top down to form a parcel. Secure with a cocktail stick.

7 Put the filled burrito in a shallow dish or casserole, cover with foil and keep warm in the oven while you make seven more. Remove the cocktail sticks before serving, sprinkled with fresh oregano.

CHICKEN FAJITAS

THE PERFECT DISH FOR CASUAL ENTERTAINING, FAJITAS ARE FLOUR TORTILLAS WHICH ARE BROUGHT TO THE TABLE FRESHLY COOKED. GUESTS ADD THEIR OWN FILLINGS BEFORE FOLDING THE TORTILLAS AND TUCKING IN.

SERVES SIX

INGREDIENTS

   3 skinless, boneless chicken breasts
   finely grated rind and juice of
     2 limes
   30ml/2 tbsp caster sugar
   10ml/2 tsp dried oregano
   2.5ml/½ tsp cayenne pepper
   5ml/1 tsp ground cinnamon
   2 onions
   3 peppers (1 red, 1 yellow or orange
     and 1 green)
   45ml/3 tbsp vegetable oil
   guacamole, salsa and soured cream,
     to serve
For the tortillas
   250g/9oz/2¼ cups plain flour, sifted
   1.5ml/¼ tsp baking powder
   pinch of salt
   50g/2oz/¼ cup lard
   60ml/4 tbsp warm water

1 Slice the chicken breasts into 2cm/¾in wide strips and place these in a large bowl. Add the lime rind and juice, caster sugar, oregano, cayenne and cinnamon. Mix thoroughly. Set aside to marinate for at least 30 minutes.

COOK'S TIP
Tortilla dough can be very difficult to roll out thinly. If the dough is breaking up try placing each ball between two sheets of clean plastic (this can be cut from a new sandwich bag). Roll out, turning over, still inside the plastic, until the tortilla is the right size.

2 Meanwhile, make the tortillas. Mix the flour, baking powder and salt in a large bowl. Rub in the lard, then add the warm water, a little at a time, to make a stiff dough. Knead this on a lightly floured surface for 10–15 minutes until it is smooth and elastic.

3 Divide the dough into 12 small balls, then roll each ball to a 15cm/6in round. Cover the rounds with plastic or clear film to keep them from drying out while you prepare the vegetables.

4 Cut the onions in half and slice them thinly. Cut the peppers in half, remove the cores and seeds, then slice the flesh into 1cm/½in wide strips.

5 Heat a large frying pan or griddle and cook each tortilla in turn for about 1 minute on each side, or until the surface colours and begins to blister. Keep the cooked tortillas warm and pliable by wrapping them in a clean, dry dish towel.

6 Heat the oil in a large frying pan. Stir-fry the marinated chicken for 5–6 minutes, then add the peppers and onions and cook for 3–4 minutes more, until the chicken strips are cooked through and the vegetables are soft and tender, but still juicy.

7 Spoon the chicken mixture into a serving bowl and take it to the table with the cooked tortillas, guacamole, salsa and soured cream. Keep the tortillas wrapped and warm.

8 To serve, each guest takes a warm tortilla, spreads it with a little salsa, adds a spoonful of guacamole and piles some of the chicken mixture in the centre. The final touch is to add a small dollop of soured cream. The tortilla is then folded over the filling and eaten in the hand.

TURKEY MOLE

A MOLE IS A RICH STEW, TRADITIONALLY SERVED ON A FESTIVE OCCASION. THE WORD COMES FROM THE AZTEC "MOLLI", MEANING A CHILLI-FLAVOURED SAUCE. THERE ARE MANY DIFFERENT TYPES, INCLUDING THE FAMOUS MOLE POBLANO DE GUAJALOTE. TOASTED NUTS, FRUIT AND CHOCOLATE ARE AMONG THE CLASSIC INGREDIENTS; THIS VERSION INCLUDES COCOA POWDER.

SERVES FOUR

INGREDIENTS

1 ancho chilli, seeded
1 guajillo chilli, seeded
115g/4oz/¾ cup sesame seeds
50g/2oz/½ cup whole blanched
  almonds
50g/2oz/½ cup shelled unsalted
  peanuts, skinned
1 small onion
2 garlic cloves
50g/2oz/¼ cup lard or 60ml/4 tbsp
  vegetable oil
50g/2oz/⅓ cup canned tomatoes in
  tomato juice
1 ripe plantain
50g/2oz/⅓ cup raisins
75g/3oz/½ cup ready-to-eat
  prunes, stoned
5ml/1 tsp dried oregano
2.5ml/½ tsp ground cloves
2.5ml/½ tsp crushed allspice berries
5ml/1 tsp ground cinnamon
25g/1oz/¼ cup cocoa powder
4 turkey breast steaks
fresh oregano, to garnish (optional)

COOK'S TIP
It is important to use good quality cocoa powder, which is unsweetened.

2 Spread out the sesame seeds in a heavy-based frying pan. Toast them over a moderate heat, shaking the pan lightly so that they turn golden all over. Do not let them burn, or the sauce will taste bitter. Set aside 45ml/3 tbsp of the toasted seeds for the garnish and tip the rest into a bowl. Toast the almonds and peanuts in the same way and add them to the bowl.

3 Chop the onion and garlic finely. Heat half the lard or oil in a frying pan, cook the chopped onion and garlic for 2–3 minutes, then add the chillies and tomatoes. Cook gently for 10 minutes.

4 Peel the plantain and slice it into short diagonal slices. Add it to the onion mixture with the raisins, prunes, dried oregano, spices and cocoa. Stir in the 250ml/8fl oz/1 cup of the reserved water in which the chillies were soaked. Bring to the boil, stirring, then add the toasted sesame seeds, almonds and peanuts. Cook for 10 minutes, stirring frequently, then remove from the heat and allow to cool slightly.

1 Soak both types of dried chilli in a bowl of hot water for 30 minutes, then lift them out and chop them roughly. Reserve 250ml/8fl oz/1 cup of the soaking liquid.

5 Blend the sauce in batches in a food processor or blender until smooth. The sauce should be fairly thick, but a little water may be added if necessary.

6 Heat the remaining lard or oil in a flameproof casserole. Add the turkey and brown over a moderate heat.

7 Pour the sauce over the steaks and cover the casserole with foil and a tight-fitting lid. Cook over a gentle heat for 20–25 minutes or until the turkey is cooked, and the sauce has thickened. Sprinkle with sesame seeds and chopped oregano, and serve with a rice dish and warm tortillas.

STUFFED LOIN OF PORK

PORK FEATURES TWICE IN THIS DELICIOUS AND LUXURIOUS DISH, WHICH CONSISTS OF A ROAST LOIN STUFFED WITH A RICH MINCED PORK MIXTURE. THE PERFECT CENTREPIECE FOR A SPECIAL OCCASION DINNER, IT IS SERVED IN MEXICO AT WEDDINGS AND SIMILAR CELEBRATIONS.

SERVES SIX

INGREDIENTS
   1.5kg/3–3½lb boneless pork loin,
      butterflied ready for stuffing
For the stuffing
   50g/2oz/⅓ cup raisins
   120ml/4fl oz/½ cup dry white wine
   15ml/1 tbsp vegetable oil
   1 onion, diced
   2 garlic cloves, crushed
   2.5ml/½ tsp ground cloves
   5ml/1 tsp ground cinnamon
   500g/1¼lb minced pork
   150ml/¼ pint/⅔ cup vegetable stock
   2 tomatoes
   50g/2oz/½ cup chopped almonds
   2.5ml/½ tsp each salt and ground
      black pepper

1 Make the stuffing. Put the raisins and wine in a bowl. Set aside. Heat the oil in a large pan, add the onion and garlic and cook for 5 minutes over a low heat.

2 Add the cloves and cinnamon, then the pork. Cook, stirring, until the pork has browned. Add the stock. Simmer, stirring frequently, for 20 minutes.

3 While the pork is simmering, peel the tomatoes. Cut a cross in the base of each tomato, then put them both in a heatproof bowl. Pour over boiling water to cover. Leave the tomatoes in the water for 3 minutes, then lift them out on a slotted spoon and plunge them into a bowl of cold water. Drain. The skins will have begun to peel back from the crosses.

4 Remove the skins completely, then chop the flesh.

5 Stir the tomatoes and almonds into the mince mixture, add the raisins and wine. Cook until the mixture has reduced to a thick sauce. Leave to cool.

6 Preheat the oven to 180°C/350°F/ Gas 4. Open out the pork loin and trim it neatly. Season the minced pork stuffing with salt and pepper to taste. Spread over the surface of the meat in a neat layer, taking it right to the edges and keeping it as even as possible.

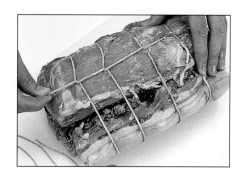

7 Roll up the pork loin carefully and tie it at intervals with kitchen string. Weigh the pork and calculate the cooking time at 30 minutes per lb/450g, plus another 30 minutes.

8 Put the stuffed pork joint in a roasting tin, season with salt and pepper and roast for the calculated time. When the joint is cooked, transfer it to a meat platter, place a tent of foil over it, and let it stand for 10 minutes before carving and serving with the roast vegetables of your choice.

COOK'S TIP
Your butcher will prepare the pork loin for you, if you give him plenty of notice.

TAMALES <u>FILLED WITH</u> SPICED PORK

THESE TAMALES ARE AMONG THE MOST ANCIENT OF MEXICAN FOODS. AT ONE TIME THE NEAT LITTLE CORN HUSK PARCELS FILLED WITH PLAIN, SAVOURY OR SWEET MASA DOUGH WERE COOKED IN THE ASHES OF A WOOD FIRE. TODAY THEY ARE MORE LIKELY TO BE STEAMED, BUT THE THRILL OF UNWRAPPING THEM REMAINS THE SAME.

SERVES SIX

INGREDIENTS
  500g/1¼lb lean pork, cut into
    5cm/2in cubes
  750ml/1¼ pints/3 cups chicken stock
  600g/1lb 6oz/4½ cups *masa harina*
  450g/1lb/2 cups lard, softened
  30ml/2 tbsp salt
  12 large or 24 small dried corn husks
  2 ancho chillies, seeded
  15ml/1 tbsp vegetable oil
  ½ onion, finely chopped
  2–3 garlic cloves, crushed
  2.5ml/½ tsp allspice berries
  2 dried bay leaves
  2.5ml/½ tsp ground cumin
  lime wedges, to serve (optional)

1 Put the pork cubes in a large saucepan. Pour over water to cover. Bring to the boil, lower the heat and simmer for 40 minutes.

2 Meanwhile, heat the chicken stock in a separate pan. Put the *masa harina* in a large bowl and add the hot stock, a little at a time, to make a stiff dough.

3 Put the lard in another bowl and beat with an electric whisk until light and fluffy, as when beating butter for a cake. Test by dropping a small amount of the whipped lard into a cup of water. If it floats, it is ready for use.

4 Continue to beat the lard, gradually adding the *masa* dough. When all of it has been added and the mixture is light and spreadable, beat in the salt. Cover closely with clear film to prevent the mixture from drying out.

5 Put the corn husks in a bowl and pour over boiling water to cover. Leave to soak for 30 minutes. Soak the seeded chillies in a separate bowl of hot water for the same time. Drain the pork, reserving 105ml/7 tbsp of the cooking liquid, and chop the meat finely.

6 Heat the oil in a large saucepan and fry the onion and garlic over a moderate heat for 2–3 minutes. Drain the chillies, chop them finely and add them to the pan. Put the allspice berries and bay leaves in a mortar, grind them with a pestle, then work in the ground cumin. Add to the onion mixture and stir well. Cook for 2–3 minutes more. Add the chopped pork and reserved cooking liquid and continue cooking over a moderate heat until all the liquid is absorbed. Leave to cool slightly.

7 Drain the corn husks and pat them dry in a clean dish towel. Place one large corn husk (or overlap two smaller ones) on a board. Spoon about one-twelfth of the *masa* mixture on to the centre of the husk wrapping and spread it almost to the sides.

8 Place a spoonful of the meat mixture on top of the *masa*. Fold the two long sides of the corn husk over the filling, then bring up each of the two shorter sides in turn, to make a neat parcel. Slide one of the two short sides inside the other, if possible, to prevent the parcel from unravelling, or tie with string or strips of the corn husk.

9 Place the *tamales* in a steamer basket over a pan of steadily simmering water and steam for 1 hour, topping up the water as needed. To test if the *tamales* are ready, unwrap one. The filling should peel away from the husk cleanly. Pile the *tamales* on a plate, leave to stand for 10 minutes, then serve with lime wedges, if liked. Guests unwrap their own *tamales* at the table.

Tacos with Shredded Beef

In Mexico tacos are most often made with soft corn tortillas, which are filled and folded in half. It is unusual to see the crisp shells of corn which are so widely used in Tex-Mex cooking. Tacos are always eaten in the hand.

3 Put the meat on a board, let it cool slightly, then shred it, using two forks. Put the meat in a bowl. Divide the tortilla dough into six equal balls.

4 Open a tortilla press and line both sides with plastic (this can be cut from a new plastic sandwich bag). Put each ball on the press and flatten it into a 15–20cm/6–8in round.

5 Heat a griddle or frying pan until hot. Cook each tortilla for 15–20 seconds on each side, and then for a further 15 minutes on the first side. Keep the tortillas warm and soft by folding them inside a slightly damp dish towel.

6 Add the oregano and cumin to the shredded meat and mix well. Heat the oil in a frying pan and fry the onion and garlic for 3–4 minutes until softened. Add the spiced meat mixture and toss over the heat until heated through.

7 Place some shredded lettuce on a tortilla, top with shredded beef and salsa, fold in half and serve with lime wedges. Garnish with fresh coriander.

SERVES SIX

INGREDIENTS
- 450g/1lb rump steak, diced
- 150g/5oz/1 cup *masa harina*
- 2.5ml/½ tsp salt
- 120ml/4fl oz/½ cup warm water
- 10ml/2 tsp dried oregano
- 5ml/1 tsp ground cumin
- 30ml/2 tbsp oil
- 1 onion, thinly sliced
- 2 garlic cloves, crushed
- fresh coriander, to garnish
- shredded lettuce, lime wedges and
  Classic Tomato Salsa, to serve

1 Put the steak in a deep frying pan and pour over water to cover. Bring to the boil, then lower the heat and simmer for 1–1½ hours.

2 Meanwhile, make the tortilla dough. Mix the *masa harina* and salt in a large mixing bowl. Add the warm water, a little at a time, to make a dough that can be worked into a ball. Knead the dough on a lightly floured surface for 3–4 minutes until smooth, then wrap the dough in clear film and leave to rest for 1 hour.

BEEF ENCHILADAS WITH RED SAUCE

ENCHILADAS ARE USUALLY MADE WITH CORN TORTILLAS, ALTHOUGH IN PARTS OF NORTHERN MEXICO FLOUR TORTILLAS ARE SOMETIMES USED.

SERVES THREE TO FOUR

INGREDIENTS

500g/1¼lb rump steak, cut into
  5cm/2in cubes
2 ancho chillies, seeded
2 pasilla chillies, seeded
2 garlic cloves, crushed
10ml/2 tsp dried oregano
2.5ml/½ tsp ground cumin
30ml/2 tbsp vegetable oil
7 fresh corn tortillas
shredded onion and flat-leaved
  parsley to garnish
salsa, to serve, optional

1 Put the steak in a deep frying pan and cover with water. Bring to the boil, then lower the heat and simmer for 1–1½ hours, or until very tender.

2 Meanwhile, put the dried chillies in a bowl and pour over the hot water. Leave to soak for 30 minutes, then tip the contents of the bowl into a blender and whizz to a smooth paste.

3 Drain the steak and let it cool, reserving 250ml/8fl oz/1 cup of the cooking liquid. Meanwhile, fry the garlic, oregano and cumin in the oil for 2 minutes.

4 Stir in the chilli paste and the reserved cooking liquid from the beef. Tear one of the tortillas into small pieces and add it to the mixture. Bring to the boil, then lower the heat. Simmer for 10 minutes, stirring occasionally, until the sauce has thickened. Shred the steak, using two forks, and stir it into the sauce, heat through for a few minutes.

5 Spoon some of the meat mixture on to each tortilla and roll it up to make an enchilada. Keep the enchiladas in a warmed dish until you have rolled them all. Garnish with shreds of onion and fresh flat-leaved parsley and then serve immediately with the salsa.

VARIATION
For a richer version place the rolled enchiladas side by side in a gratin dish. Pour over 300ml/½ pint/1¼ cups soured cream and 75g/3oz/¾ cup grated Cheddar cheese. Place under a preheated grill for 5 minutes or until the cheese melts and the sauce begins to bubble. Serve at once.

ESCABECHE

A CLASSIC DISH THAT THE MEXICANS INHERITED FROM THE SPANISH, ESCABECHE IS OFTEN CONFUSED WITH CEVICHE, WHICH CONSISTS OF MARINATED RAW FISH. IN ESCABECHE, THE RAW FISH IS INITIALLY MARINATED IN LIME JUICE, BUT IS THEN COOKED BEFORE BEING PICKLED.

SERVES FOUR

INGREDIENTS
900g/2lb whole fish fillets
juice of 2 limes
300ml/½ pint/1¼ cups olive oil
6 peppercorns
3 garlic cloves, sliced
2.5ml/½ tsp ground cumin
2.5ml/½ tsp dried oregano
2 bay leaves
50g/2oz/⅓ cup pickled jalapeño chilli
    slices, chopped
1 onion, thinly sliced
250ml/8fl oz/1 cup white wine vinegar
150g/5oz/1¼ cups green olives
    stuffed with pimiento, to garnish

1 Place the fish fillets in a single layer in a shallow non-metallic dish. Pour the lime juice over, turn the fillets over once to ensure that they are completely coated, then cover the dish and leave to marinate for 15 minutes.

2 Drain the fish in a colander, then pat the fillets dry with kitchen paper. Heat 60ml/4 tbsp of the oil in a large frying pan, add the fish fillets and sauté for 5–6 minutes, turning once, until they are golden brown. Use a fish slice to transfer them to a shallow dish that will hold them in a single layer.

3 Heat 30ml/2 tbsp of the remaining oil in a frying pan. Add the peppercorns, garlic, ground cumin, oregano, bay leaves and jalapeños, and cook over a low heat for 2 minutes, then increase the heat, add the onion slices and vinegar and bring to the boil. Lower the heat and simmer for 4 minutes.

4 Remove the pan from the heat and carefully add the remaining oil. Stir well, then pour the mixture over the fish. Leave to cool, then cover the dish and marinate for 24 hours in the fridge.

5 When you are ready to serve, drain off the liquid and garnish the pickled fish with the stuffed olives. Salad leaves would make a good accompaniment.

COOK'S TIP
Use the largest frying pan you have when cooking the fish. If your pan is too small, it may be necessary to cook them in batches. Do not overcrowd the pan as they will cook unevenly.

CEVICHE

THIS FAMOUS DISH IS PARTICULARLY POPULAR ALONG MEXICO'S WESTERN SEABOARD, IN PLACES SUCH AS ACAPULCO. IT CONSISTS OF VERY FRESH RAW FISH, "COOKED" BY THE ACTION OF LIME JUICE.

SERVES SIX

INGREDIENTS

   200g/7oz raw peeled prawns
   200g/7oz shelled scallops
   200g/7oz squid, cleaned and cut
     into serving pieces
   7 limes
   3 tomatoes
   1 small onion
   1 ripe avocado
   20ml/4 tbsp chopped fresh oregano,
     or 10ml/2 tsp dried
   5ml/1 tsp salt
   ground black pepper
   fresh oregano sprigs, to garnish
   crusty bread and lime wedges,
     to serve (optional)

1 Spread out the prawns, scallops and squid in a non-metallic bowl. Squeeze six of the limes and pour the juice over the mixed seafood to cover it completely. Cover the dish with clear film and set aside for 8 hours or overnight.

2 Drain the seafood in a colander to remove the excess lime juice, then pat it dry with kitchen paper. Place the prawns, scallops and squid in a bowl.

3 Cut the tomatoes in half, squeeze out the seeds, then dice the flesh. Cut the onion in half, then slice it thinly. Cut the avocado in half lengthways, remove the stone and peel, then cut the flesh into 1cm/½in dice.

4 Add the tomatoes, onion and avocado to the seafood with the oregano and seasoning. Squeeze the remaining lime and pour over the juice. Garnish with oregano and serve, with crusty bread and lime wedges, if liked.

SALT COD FOR CHRISTMAS EVE

THIS MEXICAN DISH IS MILDER THAN THE SIMILAR SPANISH DISH, BACALDO A LA VIZCAINA. IT IS EATEN ON CHRISTMAS EVE THROUGHOUT MEXICO.

SERVES SIX

INGREDIENTS
   450g/1lb dried salt cod
   105ml/7 tbsp extra virgin olive oil
   1 onion, halved and thinly sliced
   4 garlic cloves, crushed
   2 x 400g/14oz cans chopped
      tomatoes in tomato juice
   75g/3oz/¾ cup slivered almonds
   75g/3oz/½ cup pickled jalapeño
      chilli slices
   115g/4oz/1 cup green olives stuffed
      with pimiento
   small bunch of fresh parsley,
      finely chopped
   salt and ground black pepper
   fresh flat-leaved parsley, to garnish
   crusty bread, to serve

1 Put the cod in a large bowl and pour over enough cold water to cover. Soak for 24 hours, changing the water at least five times during this period.

2 Drain the cod and remove the skin using a large sharp knife. Shred the flesh finely using two forks, and put it into a bowl. Set it aside.

3 Heat half the oil in a large frying pan. Add the onion slices and fry over a moderate heat until the onion has softened and is translucent.

4 Remove the onion from the pan and set aside. Make sure you transfer the oil with the onion as it is an important flavouring in this dish and mustn't be discarded. In the same pan add the remaining olive oil. When the oil is hot but not smoking, add the crushed garlic and fry gently for 2 minutes.

5 Add the canned tomatoes and their juice to the pan with the garlic. Cook over a medium-high heat for about 20 minutes, stirring occasionally, until the mixture has reduced and thickened.

COOK'S TIPS
• Salt cod is available in specialist fishmongers, Spanish delicatessens and West Indian stores.
• Any leftovers can be used to fill burritos or empanadas.

6 Meanwhile, spread out the slivered almonds in a single layer in a large heavy-based frying pan. Toast them over a moderate heat for a few minutes, shaking the pan lightly throughout the process so that they turn golden brown all over. Do not let them burn.

7 Add the jalapeño chilli slices and stuffed olives to the toasted almonds.

8 Stir in the shredded fish, mixing it in thoroughly, and cook for 20 minutes more, stirring occasionally, until the mixture is almost dry.

9 Season to taste, add the parsley and cook for a further 2–3 minutes. Garnish with parsley leaves and serve in heated bowls, with crusty bread.

SALMON WITH TEQUILA CREAM SAUCE

USE REPOSADA TEQUILA, WHICH IS LIGHTLY AGED, FOR THIS SAUCE. IT HAS A SMOOTHER, MORE ROUNDED FLAVOUR, WHICH GOES WELL WITH THE CREAM.

SERVES FOUR

INGREDIENTS
   3 fresh jalapeño chillies
   45ml/3 tbsp olive oil
   1 small onion, finely chopped
   150ml/¼ pint/⅔ cup fish stock
   grated rind and juice of 1 lime
   120ml/4fl oz/½ cup single cream
   30ml/2 tbsp reposada tequila
   1 firm avocado
   4 salmon fillets
   salt and ground white pepper
   strips of green pepper and fresh flat-
      leaved parsley to garnish

1 Roast the chillies in a frying pan until the skins are blistered, being careful not to let the flesh burn. Put them in a strong plastic bag and tie the top to keep the steam in. Set aside for 20 minutes.

2 Heat 15ml/1 tbsp of the oil in a saucepan. Add the onion and fry for 3–4 minutes, then add the stock, lime rind and juice. Cook for 10 minutes, until the stock starts to reduce. Remove the chillies from the bag and peel off the skins, slit and scrape out the seeds.

3 Stir the cream into the onion and stock mixture. Slice the chilli flesh into strips and add to the pan. Cook over a gentle heat, stirring constantly, for 2–3 minutes. Season to taste with salt and white pepper.

4 Stir the tequila into the onion and chilli mixture. Leave the pan over a very low heat. Peel the avocado, remove the stone and slice the flesh. Brush the salmon fillets on one side with a little of the remaining oil.

5 Heat a frying pan or ridged grill pan until very hot and add the salmon, oiled side down. Cook for 2–3 minutes, until the underside is golden, then brush the top with oil, turn each fillet over and cook the other side until the fish is cooked and flakes easily when tested with the tip of a sharp knife.

6 Serve on a pool of sauce, with the avocado slices. Garnish with strips of green pepper and fresh parsley.

VERACRUZ-STYLE RED SNAPPER

THIS IS A CLASSIC MEXICAN DISH WHICH BORROWS BAY LEAVES AND OLIVES FROM SPAIN TO GO WITH THE NATIVE CHILLIES.

SERVES FOUR

INGREDIENTS
   4 whole red snapper, cleaned
   juice of 2 limes
   4 garlic cloves, crushed
   5ml/1 tsp dried oregano
   2.5ml/½ tsp salt
   drained bottled capers, to garnish
   lime wedges, to serve (optional)
For the sauce
   120ml/4fl oz/½ cup olive oil
   2 bay leaves
   2 garlic cloves, sliced
   4 fresh jalapeño chillies, seeded and
      cut in strips
   1 onion, thinly sliced
   8 fresh tomatoes
   75g/3oz/½ cup pickled jalapeño
      chilli slices
   15ml/1 tbsp soft dark brown sugar
   2.5ml/½ tsp ground cloves
   2.5ml/½ tsp ground cinnamon
   150g/5oz/1¼ cups green olives
      stuffed with pimiento

1 Preheat the oven to 180°C/350°F/ Gas 4. Rinse the fish inside and out, then pat dry with kitchen paper. Place in a large roasting tin in a single layer.

2 Mix the lime juice, garlic, oregano and salt in a small bowl. Pour the mixture over the fish. Bake for about 30 minutes, or until the flesh flakes easily when tested with the tip of a sharp knife.

3 Meanwhile, make the sauce. Heat the olive oil in a saucepan, add the bay leaves, garlic and chilli strips; fry over a low heat for 3–4 minutes.

4 Add the onion slices to the oil in the saucepan and cook for 3–4 minutes more, until all the onion is softened and translucent.

5 Cut a cross in the base of each tomato. Place them in a heatproof bowl and pour over boiling water to cover. After 3 minutes, lift the tomatoes out on a slotted spoon and plunge them into a bowl of cold water. Drain. The skins will have begun to peel back from the crosses.

6 Skin the tomatoes completely, then cut them in half and squeeze out the seeds. Chop the flesh finely and add it to the onion mixture. Cook for 3–4 minutes, until the tomato is starting to soften.

7 Add the pickled jalapeños, brown sugar, ground cloves and cinnamon to the sauce. Cook for 10 minutes, stirring frequently, then stir the olives into the sauce and pour a little over each fish. Garnish with the capers and serve with lime wedges, if liked. A rice dish would make a good accompaniment.

EGGS RANCHEROS

THERE ARE MANY VARIATIONS ON THIS POPULAR DISH, WHICH IS GREAT FOR BREAKFAST OR BRUNCH. THE COMBINATION OF CREAMY EGGS WITH ONION, CHILLI AND TOMATOES WORKS WONDERFULLY WELL.

SERVES FOUR FOR BREAKFAST

INGREDIENTS
2 corn tortillas, several days old
oil, for frying
2 fresh green jalapeño chillies
1 garlic clove
4 spring onions
1 large tomato
8 eggs, beaten
150ml/¼ pint/⅔ cup single cream
small bunch of fresh coriander,
  finely chopped
salt and ground black pepper

1 Cut the tortillas into long strips. Pour oil into a frying pan to a depth of 1cm/½in. Heat the oil until it is very hot, watching it closely all the time.

2 Fry the tortilla strips in batches for a minute or two until they are crisp and golden, turning them occasionally, then drain on kitchen paper.

COOK'S TIP
When cooking the tortilla strips it is important that the oil is the correct temperature. To test if the oil is ready to use, carefully add a strip of tortilla. If the strip floats and the oil immediately bubbles around its edges, the oil is ready.

3 Spear the chillies on a long-handled metal skewer and roast them over the flame of a gas burner until the skins blister and darken. Do not let the flesh burn. Alternatively, dry fry them in a griddle pan until the skins are scorched. Place them in a strong plastic bag and tie the top to keep the steam in. Set aside for 20 minutes.

4 Meanwhile, crush the garlic and chop the spring onions finely. Cut a cross in the base of the tomato. Place it in a heatproof bowl and pour over boiling water to cover. After 3 minutes lift the tomato out using a slotted spoon and plunge it into a bowl of cold water. Leave for a few minutes to cool.

5 Drain the tomato, remove the skin and cut it into four pieces. Using a teaspoon scoop out the seeds and the core, then dice the flesh finely.

6 Remove the chillies from the bag and peel off the skins. Cut off the stalks, then slit the chillies and scrape out the seeds. Chop the flesh finely. Put the eggs in a bowl, season with salt and pepper and beat lightly.

7 Heat 15ml/1 tbsp oil in a large frying pan. Add the garlic and spring onions and fry gently for 2–3 minutes until soft. Stir in the diced tomato and cook for 3–4 minutes more, then stir in the chillies and cook for 1 minute.

8 Pour the eggs into the pan and stir until they start to set. When only a small amount of uncooked egg remains visible, stir in the cream so that the cooking process is slowed down and the mixture cooks to a creamy mixture rather than a solid mass.

9 Stir the chopped coriander into the scrambled egg. Arrange the tortilla strips on four serving plates and spoon the eggs over. Serve at once.

DESSERTS,
SWEETMEATS
AND DRINKS

Mexicans love sweet things. Ever since Hernando Cortez introduced sugar cane to the country,

sweetmeats have been very much on the menu and the array of cakes and pastries in a

Mexican pastelerìa would rival any display in a European cake shop. Mexicans have some

marvellous means of slaking thirst, from refreshing fruit drinks to rich, satisfying hot chocolate, but

this chapter ends with two of the most famous of Mexico's drinks, Tequila and Margarita.

CHURROS

THESE DELECTABLE TREATS ARE TRADITIONALLY MADE BY FORCING DOUGH THROUGH A CHURRERA, WHICH IS A UTENSIL FITTED WITH A WOODEN PLUNGER. AN ICING BAG FITTED WITH A LARGE STAR NOZZLE MAKES A GOOD SUBSTITUTE. CHURROS ARE USUALLY SERVED WITH COFFEE OR HOT CHOCOLATE AND ARE PERFECT FOR DIPPING.

MAKES ABOUT TWENTY-FOUR

INGREDIENTS
  350g/12oz/3 cups plain flour
  5ml/1 tsp baking powder
  600ml/1 pint/2½ cups water
  2.5ml/½ tsp salt
  25g/1oz/3 tbsp soft dark brown sugar
  2 egg yolks
  oil, for deep frying
  2 limes, cut in wedges
  caster sugar, for dusting

COOK'S TIP
These are best eaten on the day they are made, preferably while still warm.

1 Sift the flour and baking powder into a bowl and set aside. Bring the measured water to the boil in a saucepan, add the salt and brown sugar, stirring all the time until both have dissolved. Remove from the heat, tip in all the flour and baking powder and beat the mixture continuously until smooth.

2 Beat in the egg yolks, one at a time, until the mixture is smooth and glossy. Set the batter aside to cool. Have ready a piping bag fitted with a large star nozzle which will give the *churros* their traditional shape.

3 Pour oil into a deep fryer or suitable saucepan to a depth of about 5cm/2in. Heat to 190°C/375°F, or until a cube of dried bread, added to the oil, floats and turns golden after 1 minute.

4 Spoon the batter into the piping bag. Pipe five or six 10cm/4in lengths of the mixture into the hot oil, using a knife to slice off each length as it emerges from the nozzle. Fry for 3–4 minutes or until they are golden brown. Drain the *churros* on kitchen paper while cooking successive batches, then arrange on a plate with the lime wedges, dust them with caster sugar and serve warm.

SOPAIPILLAS

THESE GOLDEN PILLOWS OF PUFF PASTRY CAN BE SERVED AS A DESSERT, WITH HONEY, OR PLAIN WITH SOUPS. THEY ARE ALSO IDEAL FOR FINGER BUFFETS.

MAKES ABOUT THIRTY

INGREDIENTS
  225g/8oz/2 cups plain flour
  15ml/1 tsp baking powder
  5ml/1 tsp salt
  25g/1oz/2 tbsp white cooking fat
    or margarine
  175ml/6fl oz/¾ cup warm water
  oil, for deep frying
  clear honey, for drizzling
  ground cinnamon for sprinkling
  crème fraîche or thick double cream,
    to serve

VARIATION
Instead of drizzling honey over the *sopaipillas*, use a mixture of 50g/2oz/ ¼ cup caster sugar and 10ml/2 tsp ground cinnamon.

1 Sift the flour, baking powder and salt into a bowl. Rub in the cooking fat or margarine until the mixture resembles fine breadcrumbs. Gradually add enough of the water to form a dough. Wrap the dough in clear film and leave for 1 hour.

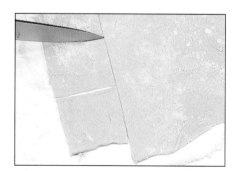

2 Working with half the dough at a time, roll it out to a square, keeping it as even and as thin as possible. Cut into 7.5cm/ 3in squares. When both pieces of the dough have been rolled and cut, set the squares aside.

3 Heat the oil for deep frying to 190°C/ 375°F, or until a cube of dried bread, added to the oil, floats and turns golden after 1 minute. Add a few pastry squares, using tongs to push them down into the oil. Cook in batches until golden on both sides, turning them once, and drain on kitchen paper.

4 When all the *sopaipillas* have been cooked, arrange on a large serving plate, drizzle with honey and sprinkle with ground cinnamon Serve warm, with crème fraîche or thick double cream.

BUÑUELOS

THESE LOVELY LITTLE PUFFS LOOK LIKE MINIATURE DOUGHNUTS AND TASTE SO GOOD IT IS HARD NOT TO OVER-INDULGE. MAKE THEM FOR BRUNCH, OR SIMPLY SERVE THEM WITH A CUP OF COFFEE OR A CUP OF HOT CHOCOLATLE.

MAKES TWELVE

INGREDIENTS
    225g/8oz/2 cups plain flour
    pinch of salt
    5ml/1 tsp baking powder
    2.5ml/½ tsp ground anise
    115g/4oz/½ cup caster sugar
    1 large egg
    120ml/4fl oz/½ cup milk
    50g/2oz/¼ cup butter
    oil, for deep frying
    10ml/2 tsp ground cinnamon
    cinnamon sticks, to decorate

1 Sift the flour, salt, baking powder and ground anise into a mixing bowl. Add 30ml/2 tbsp of the caster sugar.

2 Place the egg and milk in a small jug and whisk well with a fork. Melt the butter in a small pan.

COOK'S TIP
Buñuelos are sometimes served with syrup for dunking, although they are perfectly delicious without. To make the syrup, mix 175g/6oz/¾ cup soft dark brown sugar and 450ml/¾ pint/ scant 2 cups water in a small saucepan. Add a cinnamon stick and heat, stirring until the sugar has dissolved. Bring to the boil, then lower the heat and simmer for 15 minutes without stirring. Cool slightly before serving with the *buñuelos*.

3 Pour the egg mixture and milk gradually into the flour, stirring all the time, until well blended, then add the melted butter. Mix first with a wooden spoon and then with your hands to make a soft dough.

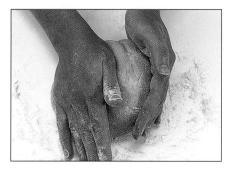

4 Lightly flour a work surface, tip out the dough on to it and knead for about 10 minutes, until smooth.

5 Divide the dough into 12 pieces and roll into balls. Slightly flatten each ball with your hand and then make a hole in the centre with the floured handle of a wooden spoon.

6 Heat the oil for deep frying to a temperature of 190ºC/375ºF, or until a cube of dried bread, added to the oil, floats and then turns a golden colour in 30–60 seconds. Fry the *buñuelos* in small batches until they are puffy and golden brown, turning them once or twice during cooking. As soon as they are golden, lift them out of the oil using a slotted spoon and lie them on a double layer of kitchen paper to drain.

7 Mix the remaining caster sugar with the ground cinnamon in a small bowl. Add the *buñuelos*, one at a time, while they are still warm, toss them in the mixture until they are lightly coated and either serve at once or leave to cool. Decorate with cinnamon sticks.

KINGS' DAY BREAD

On Twelfth Night, January 6th, Mexican children receive gifts to mark the day the Three Kings brought gifts to the infant Jesus. This sweetened rich bread, decorated with candied fruit, is an important part of the celebrations. A doll and a bean are hidden inside the cake, and the person who gets the doll has to host a party on February 2nd, another feast day. The person who finds the bean brings the drinks.

SERVES EIGHT

INGREDIENTS
    120ml/4fl oz/½ cup lukewarm water
    6 eggs
    10ml/2 tsp active dried yeast
    275g/10oz/2½ cups plain flour
    2.5ml/½ tsp salt
    50g/2oz/¼ cup granulated sugar
    115g/4oz/½ cup butter, plus 25g/1oz/
        2 tbsp melted butter, for glazing
    225g/8oz/1½ cups crystallized fruit
        and candied peel
    175g/6oz/1½ cups icing sugar, plus
        extra, for dusting
    30ml/2 tbsp single cream
    crystallized fruit and glacé cherries,
        to decorate

1 Pour the water into a small bowl, stir in the dried yeast and leave in a warm place until frothy.

2 Crack four of the eggs and divide the yolks from the whites. Place the four yolks in a small bowl and discard the egg whites.

3 Put 150g/5oz/1¼ cups of the flour in a mixing bowl. Add the salt and sugar. Break the remaining two eggs into the bowl, then add the four egg yolks.

4 Add 115g/4oz/½ cup of the butter to the bowl together with the yeast and water mixture. Mix all the ingredients together well.

5 Put the crystallized fruit and peel into a separate bowl. Add 50g/2oz/½ cup of the remaining flour and toss the fruit with the flour to coat it.

6 Add the floured fruit to the egg mixture, with the rest of the flour. Mix to a soft, non-sticky dough. Knead the dough on a lightly floured surface for about 10 minutes, until smooth.

7 Shape the dough into a ball. Using the floured handle of a wooden spoon, make a hole in the centre, and enlarge.

8 Put the dough ring onto a greased baking sheet and cover lightly with oiled clear film. Leave in a warm place for about 2 hours or until doubled in bulk.

9 Preheat the oven to 180°C/350°F/ Gas 4. Brush the dough with the melted butter and bake for about 30 minutes or until it has risen well and is cooked through and springy.

10 Mix the icing sugar and cream in a bowl. Drizzle the mixture over the bread when it is cool and decorate it with the crystallized fruit and glacé cherries. Dust with icing sugar.

PAN DULCE

THESE "SWEET BREADS" OF VARIOUS SHAPES ARE MADE THROUGHOUT MEXICO, AND ARE EATEN AS A
SNACK OR WITH JAM OR MARMALADE FOR BREAKFAST.

MAKES TWELVE

INGREDIENTS
    120ml/4fl oz/½ cup lukewarm milk
    10ml/2 tsp active dried yeast
    450g/1lb/4 cups strong plain flour
    75g/3oz/6 tbsp caster sugar
    25g/1oz/2 tbsp butter, softened
    4 large eggs, beaten
    oil, for greasing
For the topping
    75g/3oz/6 tbsp butter, softened
    115g/4oz/½ cup granulated sugar
    1 egg yolk
    5ml/1 tsp ground cinnamon
    115g/4oz/1 cup plain flour

1 Pour the milk into a small bowl, stir in the dried yeast and leave in a warm place until frothy.

2 Put the flour and sugar in a mixing bowl, add the butter and beaten eggs and mix to a soft, sticky dough.

3 Place the dough on a lightly floured surface and dredge it with more flour. Using floured hands, turn the dough over and over until it is completely covered in a light coating of flour. Cover it with lightly oiled clear film and leave to rest for 20 minutes.

4 Meanwhile, make the topping. Cream the butter and sugar in a bowl, then mix in the egg yolk, cinnamon and flour. The mixture should have a slightly crumbly texture.

5 Divide the dough into 12 equal pieces and shape each of them into a round. Space well apart on greased baking sheets. Sprinkle the topping over the breads, dividing it more or less equally among them, then press it lightly into the surface.

6 Leave the rolls in a warm place to stand for about 30 minutes until they are about one and a half times their previous size. Preheat the oven to 200°C/400°F/Gas 6 and bake the breads for about 15 minutes. Allow to cool slightly before serving.

CHRISTMAS COOKIES WITH WALNUTS

AT CHRISTMAS TIME, THESE ARE INDIVIDUALLY WRAPPED IN SMALL SQUARES OF BRIGHTLY COLOURED TISSUE PAPER AND ARRANGED IN LARGE BOWLS. FOLLOW THE MEXICANS' LEAD, AND TRANSFORM THEM INTO GIFTS BY WRAPPING FIVE OR SIX AT A TIME IN CELLOPHANE AND TYING THE PACKAGES WITH COLOURED RIBBONS.

MAKES TWENTY-FOUR

INGREDIENTS
    115g/4oz/½ cup lard
    75g/3oz/¾ cup icing sugar
    5ml/1 tsp vanilla essence
    150g/5oz/1¼ cups unbleached
      plain flour
    75g/3oz/¾ cup broken walnuts,
      finely chopped
    50g/2oz/½ cup icing sugar
    10ml/2 tsp ground cinnamon

COOK'S TIP
Polvo means "dust", and these biscuits should be crumbly and light to eat. Pecan nuts can be used instead of the walnuts, if you like.

1 Preheat the oven to 190ºC/375ºF/Gas 5. Place the lard in a large bowl and beat with an electric whisk until light and aerated.

2 Gradually beat in 25g/1oz/¼ cup of the icing sugar, then add the vanilla essence and beat well.

3 Add the flour by hand, working it gently into the mixture. Do not be tempted to use a spoon or the mixture will be too sticky. Add the walnuts and mix carefully.

4 Divide the dough evenly into 24 small pieces, roll each to a ball, and space well apart on baking sheets. Bake for 10–15 minutes, until golden, switching the baking sheets around halfway through, to ensure even baking. Cool the biscuits on wire racks.

5 Put the remaining icing sugar in a bowl and stir in the cinnamon. Add a few biscuits at a time, shaking them in the icing sugar until they are heavily coated. Shake off the excess sugar. Serve wrapped in coloured paper.

MEXICAN WEDDING COOKIES

*ALMOST HIDDEN BENEATH THEIR VEIL OF ICING SUGAR, THESE LITTLE SHORTBREAD BISCUITS ARE
TRADITIONALLY SERVED AT WEDDINGS, AND ARE ABSOLUTELY DELICIOUS. SERVE THEM AFTER DINNER
WITH COFFEE AND PERHAPS A GLASS OF THE MEXICAN COFFEE LIQUEUR – KAHLÚA.*

MAKES THIRTY

INGREDIENTS
  225g/8oz/1 cup butter, softened
  175g/6oz/1½ cups icing sugar
  5ml/1 tsp natural vanilla essence
  300g/11oz/2¾ cups plain flour
  pinch of salt
  150g/5oz/1¼ cups pecan nuts,
    finely chopped

1 Preheat the oven to 190°C/375°F/
Gas 5. Beat the butter in a large bowl
until it is light and fluffy, then beat in
115g/4oz/1 cup of the icing sugar, with
the vanilla essence.

2 Gradually add the flour and salt to the
creamed mixture until it starts to form a
dough. Add the finely chopped pecans
with the remaining flour. Knead the
dough lightly.

3 Divide the dough into 30 equal pieces
and roll them into balls. Space about
5mm/¼in apart on baking sheets. Press
each ball lightly with your thumb, to
flatten it slightly.

4 Bake the biscuits for 10–15 minutes
until they are starting to brown. Cool on
the baking sheets for 10 minutes, then
transfer to wire racks to cool completely.

5 Put the remaining icing sugar in a
bowl. Add a few biscuits at a time,
shaking them in the icing sugar until
they are heavily coated. Serve straight-
away or store in an airtight tin.

ALMOND ORANGE BISCUITS

*THE COMBINATION OF LARD AND ALMONDS GIVES THESE BISCUITS A LOVELY SHORT TEXTURE, SO THAT
THEY MELT IN THE MOUTH. THEY ARE PERFECT WITH COFFEE OR HOT CHOCOLATE.*

MAKES THIRTY-SIX

INGREDIENTS
  250g/9oz/generous 1 cup lard
  125g/4½oz/generous ½ cup
    caster sugar
  2 eggs, beaten
  grated rind and juice of
    1 small orange
  300g/11oz/1¾ cups plain flour,
    sifted with 5ml/1 tsp baking powder
  200g/7oz/1¾ cups ground almonds
For dusting
  50g/2oz/½ cup icing sugar
  5ml/1 tsp ground cinnamon

COOK'S TIP
If you can't be bothered to roll out the
dough, just divide it into 36 pieces and
roll each one into a ball. Place these on
baking sheets and flatten each one into
a biscuit shape with a fork.

1 Preheat the oven to 200°C/400°F/
Gas 6. Place the lard in a large bowl
and beat with an electric whisk until
light and aerated. Gradually beat in the
caster sugar.

2 Continue to whisk the mixture while
you add the eggs, orange rind and
juice. Whisk for 3–4 minutes more, then
stir in the flour mixture and ground
almonds to form a dough.

3 Roll out the dough on a lightly floured
surface until it is about 1cm/½in thick.
Using biscuit cutters, cut out 36 rounds,
re-rolling the dough if necessary. Gently
lift the rounds on to baking sheets.

4 Bake for about 10 minutes, or until
the biscuits are golden. Leave to stand
on the baking sheets for 10 minutes to
cool and firm slightly.

5 Mix together the icing sugar and
cinnamon. Put the mixture in a small
sieve or tea strainer and dust the
biscuits well. Leave to cool completely.

CAPIROTADA

MEXICAN COOKS BELIEVE IN MAKING GOOD USE OF EVERYTHING AVAILABLE TO THEM. THIS PUDDING WAS INVENTED AS A WAY OF USING UP FOOD BEFORE THE LENTEN FAST, BUT IS NOW EATEN AT OTHER TIMES TOO.

SERVES SIX

INGREDIENTS
1 small French stick, a few days old
75–115g/3–4oz/⅓–½ cup butter, softened, plus extra for greasing
200g/7oz/scant 1 cup soft dark brown sugar
1 cinnamon stick, about 15cm/ 6in long
400ml/14fl oz/1⅔ cups water
45ml/3 tbsp dry sherry
75g/3oz/¾ cup flaked almonds, plus extra, to decorate
75g/3oz/½ cup raisins
115g/4oz/1 cup grated Monterey Jack or mild Cheddar cheese
single cream, for pouring

1 Slice the bread into about 30 rounds, each 1cm/½in thick. Lightly butter on both sides. Cook in batches in a warm frying pan until browned, turning over once. Set the slices aside.

2 Place the sugar, cinnamon stick and water in a saucepan. Heat gently, stirring all the time, until the sugar has dissolved. Bring to the boil, then lower the heat and simmer for 15 minutes without stirring. Remove the cinnamon stick, then stir in the sherry.

COOK'S TIP
This recipe works well with older bread that is quite dry. If you only have fresh bread, slice it and dry it out for a few minutes in a low oven.

3 Preheat the oven to 180°C/350°F/ Gas 4. Grease a 20cm/8in square baking dish with butter. Layer the bread rounds, almonds, raisins and cheese in the dish, pour the syrup over, letting it soak into the bread. Bake the pudding for about 30 minutes until golden brown.

4 Remove from the oven, leave to stand for 5 minutes, then cut into squares. Serve cold, with single cream poured over and decorated with the extra flaked almonds.

DRUNKEN PLANTAIN

MEXICANS ENJOY THEIR NATIVE FRUITS AND UNTIL THEIR CUISINE WAS INFLUENCED BY THE SPANISH AND THE FRENCH, THEY HAD NO PASTRIES OR CAKES, PREFERRING TO END THEIR MEALS WITH FRUIT, WHICH WAS ABUNDANT. THIS DESSERT IS QUICK AND EASY TO PREPARE, AND TASTES DELICIOUS.

SERVES SIX

INGREDIENTS
3 ripe plantains
50g/2oz/¼ cup butter, diced
45ml/3 tbsp rum
grated rind and juice of 1 small orange
5ml/1 tsp ground cinnamon
50g/2oz/¼ cup soft dark brown sugar
50g/2oz/½ cup whole almonds, in their skins
fresh mint sprigs, to decorate
Crème fraîche or thick double cream, to serve

1 Preheat the oven to 180°C/350°F/ Gas 4. Peel the plantains and cut them in half lengthways. Put the pieces in a shallow baking dish, dot them all over with butter, then spoon over the rum and orange juice.

2 Mix the orange rind, cinnamon and brown sugar in a bowl. Sprinkle the mixture over the plantains.

3 Bake for 25–30 minutes, until the plantains are soft and the sugar has melted into the rum and orange juice to form a sauce.

4 Meanwhile, slice the almonds and dry fry them in a heavy-based frying pan until the cut sides are golden. Serve the plantains in individual bowls, with some of the sauce spooned over. Sprinkle the almonds on top, decorate with the fresh mint sprigs and offer crème fraîche or double cream separately.

TEQUILA

THERE ARE SEVERAL DIFFERENT TYPES OF TEQUILA, MEXICO'S NATIONAL SPIRIT. EACH TYPE OF TEQUILA IS AVAILABLE IN SEVERAL DIFFERENT BRANDS, EACH WITH A DISTINCTIVE FLAVOUR INFLUENCED BY THE SOIL TYPE, SUGAR CONTENT OF THE AGAVE PLANTS, CLIMATE, COOKING AND FERMENTING PROCESS.

There are many different ways of serving tequila. Perhaps the best known of these is the slammer, when shots of chilled tequila are drunk with salt and lime. *Joven* (young) or *reposada* (rested) tequila is often served at room temperature in small shot glasses called *caballitos*, and sipped slowly so that all the flavours can be savoured. *Anejo* (aged) tequila should be served in a small balloon glass (a large glass would allow too much of the aroma to escape). It can be diluted with a little water, but ice should not be added.

TEQUILA SLAMMERS
Mexicans have long enjoyed the taste of lime and salt with their food and drink. Beer is also taken with lime and salt.

INGREDIENTS
 chilled tequila
 salt
 wedges of lime

HOW TO SERVE TEQUILA
Pour a shot glass of tequila. Lick the space between the thumb and the index finger on your left hand, then sprinkle this area with salt. Taking care not to spill the salt, hold a lime wedge in the same hand. Pick up the shot glass in your right hand. Lick the salt, down the tequila in one, suck the lime, then slam down your empty glass. Some drinkers manage salt, lime and tequila in the same hand, but this takes practice.

MARGARITA

THE MOST RENOWNED TEQUILA COCKTAIL, THIS CAN BE SERVED OVER ICE CUBES OR "FROZEN" –
MIXED WITH CRUSHED ICE IN A COCKTAIL SHAKER TO CREATE A LIQUID SORBET EFFECT,
THEN POURED INTO THE GLASS.

SERVES ONE

INGREDIENTS
   45ml/3 tbsp tequila
   25ml/1½ tbsp triple sec
   25ml/1½ tbsp freshly squeezed
     lime juice
  crushed ice or ice cubes
  lime wedge and salt, for
    frosting glass

COOK'S TIP
White tequila is the traditional spirit to
use, but today many people prefer to
make margaritas with reposada tequila,
which gives a more rounded flavour.

1 Frost a cocktail glass by rubbing the
outer rim with the wedge of lime. Dip
the glass in a saucer of salt so that it is
evenly coated. It is important that there
is no salt inside the glass, so take care
that lime juice is only applied to the
outer rim.

2 Combine the tequila, triple sec and
lime juice in a cocktail shaker, add
crushed ice, if using, and shake to mix.
Carefully pour into the frosted glasses.
If crushed ice is not used, place ice
cubes in the glass and then pour the
mixture over.

INDEX

New
Headway
Pronunciation

Pre-Intermediate
Student's Practice Book

Bill Bowler
Sue Parminter

OXFORD
UNIVERSITY PRESS

Contents

Introduction

Welcome to the *New Headway Pre-Intermediate Pronunciation Course*!

The questions and answers on these pages are to help you to understand this book, so that you can get the best out of it when you use it.

Who is this book for?

The *New Headway Pre-Intermediate Pronunciation Course* is for pre-intermediate students who wish to improve their pronunciation.

How does this book work?

You can use this book (and recording) on its own. The exercises in it will help you to organize your study of pronunciation.

It is also part of the *New Headway English Course* and the topics and language of each unit in this book link with those in the *New Headway Pre-Intermediate Student's Book*.

Sounds exercises

		All nationalities	Arabic	Chinese	Czech	French	German	Greek	Hungarian	Italian	Japanese	Polish	Portuguese	Russian	Spanish	Turkish
Unit 1	Consonant symbols 1: the easily recognizable phonemic symbols /p/, /b/, /t/, /d/, /k/, /g/, /f/, /v/, /s/, /z/, /h/, /l/, /r/, /m/, /n/, and /w/ – voiced and voiceless consonants	✓														
Unit 2	The sounds /s/, /z/, and /ɪz/	✓														
Unit 3	Pronunciation of -*ed* past tenses	✓														
Unit 4	Single vowel symbols /iː/, /ɪ/, /ɜː/, /ə/, /uː/, /ʊ/, /ɑː/, /ʌ/, /ɔː/, /ɒ/, /e/, and /æ/ – long and short vowels	✓														
Unit 5	The sound /w/		✓	✓		✓	✓	✓	✓		✓	✓		✓	✓	✓
Unit 6	The sounds /n/ and /ŋ/, and /ŋg/ and /ndʒ/					✓	✓	✓	✓	✓	✓		✓		✓	✓
Unit 7	Consonant symbols 2: the less easily recognizable phonemic symbols /ʃ/, /ʒ/, /tʃ/, /dʒ/, /θ/, /ð/, /j/, and /ŋ/ – voiced and voiceless consonants	✓														
Unit 8	The sounds /ʃ/, /s/, and /tʃ/		✓	✓		✓	✓	✓	✓	✓			✓		✓	
	The sounds /ʊ/ and /uː/				✓	✓	✓	✓	✓	✓	✓	✓	✓		✓	✓
Unit 9	The sounds /iː/ and /ɪ/				✓	✓	✓	✓	✓	✓	✓	✓			✓	✓
Unit 10	'Double vowel' or diphthong symbols /eɪ/, /aɪ/, /ɔɪ/, /ɪə/, /eə/, /əʊ/, /aʊ/, and /ʊə/	✓														
Unit 11	The sounds /e/, /æ/, and /ʌ/	✓														
Unit 12	The sounds /e/ and /eɪ/	✓														
Unit 13	The sound /h/					✓	✓	✓		✓	✓		✓		✓	✓
Unit 14	The sounds /ɒ/, /ɔː/, and /əʊ/	✓														

What types of exercise are there?

There are five different types of exercise in this book:

1 **Sounds and sound symbols** The sounds exercises help you to practise the sounds we use in English. Some sounds exercises are very useful for speakers of specific languages. (See the table opposite.)

2 **Sounds and sound symbols exercises** Sound symbols exercises teach English sound symbols (phonemic symbols). The connection between English spelling and pronunciation is a problem for speakers of all languages. Knowing English phonemic symbols helps you to learn the pronunciation of new words easily.

   As you learn the symbols, you write example words in the chart on page 55. This helps you to remember the phonemic symbols correctly.

3 **Connected speech** These exercises help you to pronounce words in phrases and sentences correctly.

4 **Intonation and sentence stress** These exercises help you to hear and practise different kinds of intonation and sentence stress patterns.

5 **Word focus** In these exercises you study groups of words where there are problems with sounds and word stress.

What about the recording?

This book comes with one tape or CD.

The symbol in the exercise shows exactly which part of the recording you listen to.

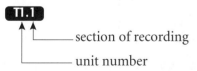
section of recording
unit number

What about the key?

The answers to exercises, and tapescripts which are not in full in the exercises themselves, are in the key at the back of the book.

As in the *New Headway Student's Book*, sometimes we ask you questions to help you work out rules for yourself. The answers to these questions are in the key, too.

This symbol after an exercise means look at the key. The page number with the symbol shows you exactly where to look.

 p56

What about technical words?

Here is a list of technical words we use in this book. Use a bilingual dictionary to translate them. You can look back at this list while you use the book.

consonant _____

contraction _____

formal _____

impolite _____

informal _____

intonation _____

linking _____

phonemic _____

pronunciation _____

rhythm _____

sound _____

spelling _____

stress _____

syllable _____

symbol _____

voiced _____

voiceless _____

vowel _____

weak _____

1

Consonant symbols 1
Word linking
Intonation in *Wh-* and *Yes/No* questions

Sound symbols

Consonant symbols 1

- These words contain the letter *c*, but the pronunciation of the letter is different in each word.

 Listen.

communicate   faces   ancient

- These words all contain the same sound, but the spelling of the sound is different in each word.

T1.2 Listen.

communicate   technology   speaking

- Looking at the spelling of English words does not always help you to pronounce them correctly. This is why sound symbols, or 'phonemic symbols', are important.

  If you write a word in sound symbols, you write what you hear. /k/, for example, is the sound in *communicate*, *technology*, and *speaking*. If you can read sound symbols, you can look up the pronunciation of words in a dictionary.

  In this book, you will learn all the English phonemic symbols. In this unit you will learn most of the symbols for consonant sounds.

1 Write these words on the sound symbol lines below, according to the sound of the underlined letters.

go	drive	play
van	letter	book
room	mean	flat
can	music	never
study	teacher	
work	hot	

/p/   **play**

/b/ _____

/t/ _____

/d/ _____

/k/ _____

/g/ _____

/f/ _____

/v/ _____

/s/ _____

/z/ _____

/h/ _____

/l/ _____

/r/ _____

/m/ _____

/n/ _____

/w/ _____

T1.3 Listen and check your answers.

▶▶ p56

2 `T1.4` Now listen to the sound symbols on their own. What is the difference in sound between the symbols in Picture A and those in Picture B? Match the pictures with the diagrams below.

/p/ /t/ /k/ /f/ /s/ /h/

/b/ /d/ /g/ /v/ /z/ /l/ /r/ /m/ /n/ /w/

Picture A   Picture B

Diagram 1   Diagram 2

▶▶ p56

3 `T1.5` Do the sound symbols in **Y** match the sound of the letters <u>underlined</u> in the words in **X**? Listen and mark the symbols ✓ if they match and ✗ if they don't match.

	X	Y	
1	<u>wh</u>y	/h/	✗
2	<u>wh</u>o	/h/	✓
3	uni<u>qu</u>e	/k/	
4	<u>sc</u>issors	/sk/	
5	<u>c</u>ity	/s/	
6	<u>ph</u>one	/ph/	
7	<u>kn</u>ow	/n/	
8	<u>v</u>ery	/v/	
9	<u>qu</u>ickly	/kw/	
10	adverti<u>s</u>ing	/s/	
11	ar<u>ch</u>itect	/k/	
12	<u>wr</u>ite	/wr/	

Correct the sound symbols that don't match.

▶▶ p56

4 Turn to the Sound symbol chart on p55. Write in an example word to help you remember each sound symbol you now know. Underline the letters in the word that match the sound symbol.

Example

/p/
<u>p</u>eo<u>p</u>le

Connected speech

Word linking

1 `T1.6` Listen. How many words do you hear in each sentence? Contractions count as two words.

Example It's¹² a³ nice⁴ big⁵ place.⁶ = 6 words

1 ☐ 2 ☐ 3 ☐ 4 ☐ 5 ☐

▶▶ p56

2 `T1.7` Listen to these two phrases.

ΑΒΓΔΕΖΗΘΙΚΛΜ
αβγδεζηθικλμ
ΝΞΟΠΡΣΤΥΦΧΨΩ
νξοπρστυφχψω

Greek‿alphabet

From:	Jack
To:	Rose
Subject:	Greetings
Date:	Tuesday

Dear Rose,
Just a quick email to say 'hi'.
Love,
Jack.

modern‿email

- When we speak quickly, a word that begins with a vowel sound is linked to the consonant sound at the end of the word before it:

  Greek_alphabet   modern_email

- Linking also happens if a consonant is usually silent at the end of a word:

  /w/   /r/
  new_idea   computer_information

- The letter y links to the following vowel sound as a /j/:

  /j/
  14th-century_English

3 **T1.8** Listen and practise saying these three phrases, paying attention to the linking.

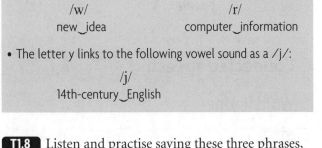

new_idea

14th-century_English

computer_information

4 **T1.9** Listen and then practise saying all the five phrases in the same way, starting from the end.

5 Mark the links in these phrases.

> a message_in_a bottle
>
> anger and other emotions
>
> a lot of information
>
> How is it possible?
>
> quickly and easily
>
> words on a page

T1.10 Listen and check your answers.

▶▶ p56

6 Listen again and practise saying the phrases, paying attention to the linking.

Intonation and sentence stress

Intonation in *Wh-* and *Yes/No* questions

- There are two basic kinds of question.

- *Wh-* questions contain a question word (*Who, What, Where, Why, How,* etc.). These questions ask for information answers.

- *Yes/No* questions do not contain question words. These questions ask for *Yes* or *No* answers.

1 Look at the questions below. Mark the *Wh-* questions with a star (*).

1 Where do you live, _____ ?

2 When's your birthday, _____ ?

3 Do you have a job, _____ ?

4 What sort of music do you like, _____ ?

5 Have you got any brothers or sisters, _____ ?

6 Can you speak three languages, _____ ?

7 How do you come to school, _____ ?

8 Do you like dancing, _____ ?

▶▶ p56

2 **T1.11** Listen to the recording and mark these statements **True** or **False**. (The names at the end of the questions will help you to hear the intonation more clearly.)

> 1 The voice goes up at the end of *Wh-* questions.
> _____
>
> 2 The voice goes up at the end of *Yes/No* questions.
> _____

▶▶ p56

3 Listen again and repeat the questions and the names. (Use your memory. Don't write the names in the gaps in 1.)

 Make sure your intonation goes clearly up or down on the name, according to whether you are asking a *Yes/No* or a *Wh-* question.

4 Now complete each question in 1 with the name of a student in your class. (Put a different name in each question.)

Listen again and repeat the questions. Say the names you have written instead of the names on the recording. If there are questions you don't like, cross them out and write your own questions. Practise saying them with the correct intonation.

5 Stand up and walk round the classroom. Ask each classmate the question you have prepared for him/her. Write down the answers you get.

When you finish, tell your teacher about your classmates.

2

The sounds /s/, /z/, and /ɪz/
Two-syllable nouns
Strong and weak forms of auxiliary verbs

Sounds

The sounds /s/, /z/, and /ɪz/

1 Read the passage about Irene Redmond.
Which adjectives do you think describe her life?

| sad | lonely | easy | boring | busy |

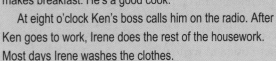

Irene Redmond and her husband Ken
live in Hamilton Gate in Queensland,
Australia. They have three children.

In the summer, when it's hot,
Irene <u>gets</u> up at six o'clock and <u>tries</u>
to do all the housework by eight. Ken
makes breakfast. He's a good cook.

At eight o'clock Ken's boss calls him on the radio. After
Ken goes to work, Irene does the rest of the housework.
Most days Irene <u>washes</u> the clothes.

At ten o'clock Irene puts the baby to bed and teaches her
eldest daughter. Usually she manages to do two hours of
classes a day with her. They eat at twelve. Irene always
bakes her own bread and cakes. She doesn't go shopping,
but orders food on the Internet. In the afternoon she spends
time with the children.

The nearest town is Tibooburra. It's 100 miles away. Irene
isn't lonely, but she misses her family. Sometimes she drives
into Tibooburra to see a friend. The nearest neighbour lives
35 miles away. She invites him to tea every week.

In the evening Irene surfs the Internet, reads or plays
cards with Ken. Usually Ken loses. They don't have a TV.

Irene likes living in Hamilton Gate. Ken loves it and hopes
to stay there for the rest of his life, but Irene isn't sure.

2 Work on your own. Read the passage again and
underline all the verbs in the third person singular of
the Present Simple except *is*, *doesn't*, and *isn't*.

3 Work with a partner. Put the verbs you underlined into
three groups, according to the pronunciation of the
third person ending.

Group 1 /s/	**Group 2** /z/	**Group 3** /ɪz/
get<u>s</u>	trie<u>s</u>	wash<u>es</u>

T2.1 Listen and check your answers.

▶▶ p56

4 Listen again and repeat the verbs, paying attention to
the pronunciation of the ending.

5 Circle the correct pronunciation to complete the rules.

1 You pronounce the ending /s/ /z/ /ɪz/ if the verb ends in
   one of the following sounds:

   /s/ **Example** mi<u>ss</u>   /tʃ/ **Example** wat<u>ch</u>

   /z/ **Example** lo<u>s</u>e   /dʒ/ **Example** mana<u>g</u>e

   /ʃ/ **Example** wa<u>sh</u>

2 If the verb ends in any other voiceless consonant sound,
   you pronounce the ending /s/ /z/ /ɪz/. **Example** makes

3 If the verb ends in any other voiced consonant sound or
   a vowel sound, you pronounce the ending /s/ /z/ /ɪz/.
   Example rains

▶▶ p56

6 Work with a partner. How much of the passage can
you remember? Use the verb lists from 3 to make
sentences about Irene's life.

Pay attention to the pronunciation of the verb endings.

Word focus

Two-syllable nouns

1 **T2.2** Diane DeVine is a film star. Listen to her and one of her fans.

2 She has lots of likes and dislikes. Match these words with the pictures below.

champagne	Japan	trumpets	shampoo
paintings	coffee	guitars	apples
sardines	cartoons	Britain	toothpaste

3 Why does Diane DeVine like the objects on the left? (Think of her name.)

T2.3 Listen and check your answers.

►► p56

Listen again and repeat the words, paying attention to stress.

4 Look at the nouns below and make sure you know what they mean. Which are stressed ● ● and which ● ● ?

T2.4 Listen and mark the stresses.

● ●			
zebras	mountains	climate	diamonds
giraffes	country	football	descent
baseball	exports	reserve	swimming

Which is the usual stress pattern for two-syllable nouns?

►► p56

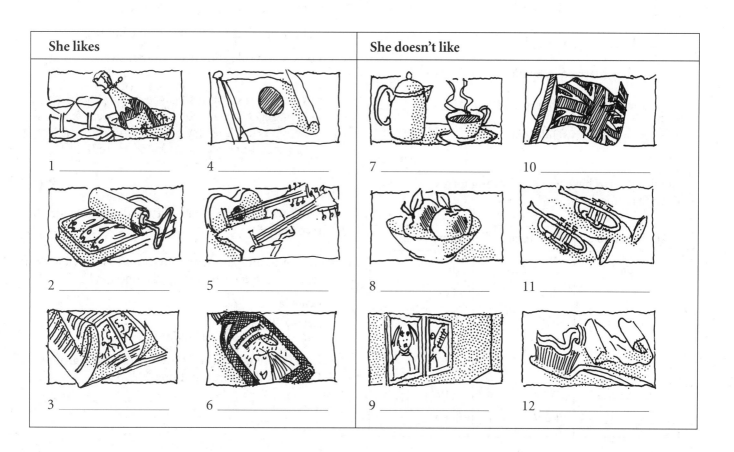

She likes	She doesn't like
1 _____ 4 _____	7 _____ 10 _____
2 _____ 5 _____	8 _____ 11 _____
3 _____ 6 _____	9 _____ 12 _____

Connected speech

Strong and weak forms of auxiliary verbs

1 Read the text about Janet Stobbs and her husband Eduardo Revuelta.

> Janet and Eduardo Revuelta-Stobbs live near Alicante in Spain. They were married in Alicante. Eduardo's a doctor and Janet's an English teacher. Janet was born in England, but she can speak good Spanish. They share the housework. Eduardo likes cooking. They've got two children – Arturo and Pablo.

2 Answer these questions. Use short answers.

1 Does Janet live in Spain? **Yes, she does.**

2 Has she got a job? _____

3 Was she born in England? _____

4 Can she speak Spanish? _____

5 Were they married in Spain? _____

6 Do they share the housework? _____

7 Have they got any children? _____

►► p56

3 Auxiliary verbs have weak and strong forms. Complete this table.

Auxiliary verb	Weak form	Strong form
_____do_____	/də/ or /dʊ/	/duː/
_____	/dəz/	/dʌz/
_____	/həv/	/hæv/
_____	/həz/	/hæz/
_____	/wə/	/wɜː/
_____	/wəz/	/wɒz/
_____	/kən/	/kæn/

►► p57

4 **T2.5** Listen to the questions and answers in 2. Underline the weak forms like this ‿ and the strong forms like this ___ .

►► p57

5 **T2.6** Listen. If you hear the weak form of the auxiliary, write **W**. If you hear the strong form, write **S**.

1 Was your plane late? **W**
It was very late. **W**

2 Have you got a new coat? ☐
Yes, I have. ☐

3 Does your girlfriend work with you? ☐
Yes, she does. ☐

4 Were they married in Mexico? ☐
No, they were married in New York. ☐

5 Has your father got grey hair? ☐
Yes, he has. ☐

6 Do you go jogging every day? ☐
Yes, I do. ☐

7 How many languages can you speak? ☐
I can speak two – English and Chinese. ☐

Look at the rule and check your answers.

> We use the weak form when the auxiliary verb is at the beginning or in the middle of a sentence, and when it is not stressed. We use the strong form when the auxiliary verb is at the end of a sentence, or stressed.

►► p57

6 Work with a partner. Practise the dialogues with the recording.

7 In groups, prepare seven questions to interview your teacher. Use each auxiliary verb once.

Example
Have you got a car?
Has your car got a CD player?

Interview your teacher. Listen to the other groups. Don't ask the same questions!

3

Pronunciation of *-ed* past tenses
Saying years
Strong and weak forms of prepositions of time and place

Sounds

Pronunciation of *-ed* past tenses

1 **T3.1** Listen to the beginnings of three stories. Notice the way the *-ed* verb endings are pronounced.

1 Last night Bert stopped at the supermarket on his way home.
2 Yesterday afternoon Fred called a restaurant to book a table for two.
3 Yesterday evening David invited Amanda to dinner.

2 **T3.2** The rest of the stories are mixed up. Listen as you read, and sort the sentences into columns, according to the pronunciation of the *-ed* verb endings.

4 He arranged a meeting with his daughter there.
5 He cooked a big supper for his wife and children.
6 He decided to cook her favourite meal.
7 He washed up after supper.
8 They ordered a lot of the most expensive things on the menu.
9 They watched a good film on TV after the meal.
10 They enjoyed it a lot.
11 The food was wasted because she didn't come.
12 They arrived home after midnight.

Bert /t/	Fred /d/	David /ɪd/
1	2	3

►► p57

Who had the worst evening, do you think?

Here are the rules for the pronunciation of the *-ed* endings:

- If the verb ends in the sound /t/ or /d/, we pronounce the *-ed* ending /ɪd/. **Example** *invited* /ɪnˈvaɪtɪd/.

- If the verb ends in a **voiced consonant sound** apart from /d/ (/b/, /g/, /v/, /z/, /ð/, /ʒ/, /dʒ/, /l/, /m/, /n/, /ŋ/), or a vowel, we pronounce the *-ed* ending /d/. **Example** *called* /kɔːld/.

- If the verb ends in a **voiceless consonant sound** apart from /t/ (/p/, /k/, /f/, /s/, /θ/, /ʃ/ or /tʃ/), we pronounce the *-ed* ending /t/. **Example** *stopped* /stɒpt/.

3 Check the meaning and pronunciation of these verbs in a dictionary.

answer	laugh	show	believe
walk	mend	try	start
plan	watch	wash	carry

4 Write the past tense form of each verb in the correct column below. (Take care with the spelling!)

/t/	/d/	/ɪd/
	answered	

T3.3 Listen and check your answers.

►► p57

Sometimes it is difficult to hear the difference between the /t/ and /d/ endings. When the verb is linked to the next word because that word starts with a vowel sound, the endings are much clearer.

5 **T3.4** Listen to the linking.

/t/
She laughed‿at the joke.

T3.5 Listen and mark the links in these sentences.

4 He tried a piece.

1 She walked all day.

5 They planned it weeks ago.

2 We watched it carefully.

6 It washed all the glasses beautifully.

▶▶ p57

Listen again and practise the sentences, paying attention to the linking.

3 They answered everybody's questions.

Word focus

Saying years

1 Circle the correct date in each of these sentences. (If you don't know the answers, try to guess them.)

History Quiz

1 Christopher Columbus discovered America in **1492** **1713**.

2 William Shakespeare died in **1840** **1616**.

3 The First World War ended in **1780** **1918**.

4 East and West Germany became one country again in **1990** **1900**.

5 The Second World War began in **1939** **1410**.

6 Napoleon Bonaparte lost the Battle of Waterloo in **1314** **1815**.

7 John F Kennedy became President of the United States in **1504** **1960**.

T3.6 Listen and check your answers.

►► p57

2 Write these dates in words.

1 **1314** = thirteen fourteen

2 *1410* = _____

3 **1492** = _____

4 *1504* = _____

5 *1616* = _____

6 1713 = _____

7 **1780** = _____

8 **1815** = _____

9 *1840* = _____

10 **1900** = _____

11 **1918** = _____

12 1939 = _____

13 **1960** = _____

14 1990 = _____

T3.7 Listen and check your answers. Listen again and mark the stress.

What happens to the stress in the *-teen* words?

►► p57

3 Work in three teams. Think of other dates in the history of your country or the world. Write a History Quiz and then test the other teams.

Score like this:

+15 points for a correct date

+10 points for the nearest guess

−5 points for incorrect pronunciation of the dates

Connected speech

Strong and weak forms of prepositions

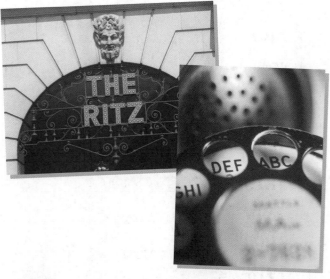

1 **T3.8** Listen to this conversation between James Bond's boss, M, and his secretary, Miss Moneypenny. As you listen, fill in the missing prepositions.

B Hello. Can I speak (1) __to__ Miss Moneypenny?

S Speaking.

B Hello, M here. I'm phoning (2) _____ the Ritz. I'm looking (3) _____ James Bond. We had a lunch appointment (4) _____ twelve. Is he there?

S I'm sorry, sir, but he's gone (5) _____ Budapest.

B I was afraid (6) _____ that. Where exactly?

S He's staying (7) _____ the Hotel Royal.

B Why didn't he listen (8) _____ me? He's just asking (9) _____ trouble.

S He's only staying there (10) _____ a couple (11) _____ days.

B All right. Contact him and tell him (12) _____ me he's a damn fool. Oh, and you can tell him I'm waiting (13) _____ his call.

S Yes, sir.

What do you notice about the pronunciation of these prepositions?

▶▶ p57

2 Look back at the dialogue and complete each phrase below with a preposition.

_____	Miss Moneypenny
	Budapest
	me

| _____ | the Ritz |
| | me |

_____	James Bond
	trouble
	a couple
	his call

| appointment | _____ | twelve |
| staying | | the Hotel Royal |

| afraid | _____ | that |
| couple | | days |

3 **T3.9** Listen and practise saying the prepositions on their own and in the phrases.

4 Read the dialogue aloud with a partner. Pronounce the prepositions in their weak forms.

4 Single vowel symbols
Containers
List intonation

Sound symbols

Single vowel symbols

In this unit you will learn the phonemic symbols for single vowel sounds.

1 **T4.1** Listen to the symbols below. What is the difference between the symbols in Picture A and the symbols in Picture B?

/iː/ /ɜː/ /uː/ /ɑː/ /ɔː/

/ɪ/ /ə/ /ʊ/ /ʌ/ /ɒ/ /e/ /æ/

Picture A   **Picture B**

▶▶ p57

2 **T4.2** Listen to the sound symbols and write in the example words.

1 /iː/   _____teacher_____   7 /ɑː/ _____

2 /ɪ/ _____   8 /ʌ/ _____

3 /ɜː/ _____   9 /ɔː/ _____

4 /ə/ _____   10 /ɒ/ _____

5 /uː/ _____   11 /e/ _____

6 /ʊ/ _____   12 /æ/ _____

▶▶ p57

3 Underline the letters in the words which match the sound symbols.

▶▶ p57

- It is important to learn these vowel symbols, because English spelling doesn't always help with the pronunciation of words.

- The same letters can have different vowel sounds:

  soup   couple   bought
  /uː/   /ʌ/   /ɔː/

- Different letters can have the same vowel sound:

  soup   boots   suit
  /uː/   /uː/   /uː/

4 **T4.3** Listen and cross out the word which does not contain the vowel sound on the left.

1 /e/   bread   wom<u>a</u>n   eggs   m<u>a</u>ny
2 /ʌ/   en<u>ough</u>   br<u>o</u>ther   sugar   much
3 /ɒ/   <u>o</u>nion   c<u>o</u>ffee   lot   what
4 /ɜː/   shirt   pork   world   univ<u>e</u>rsity
5 /iː/   cheese   tea   wine   magaz<u>i</u>nes
6 /ɑː/   car   c<u>a</u>rrots   half   aren't
7 /ɪ/   buildings little   birds   milk
8 /uː/   shamp<u>oo</u> look   fruit   two

▶▶ p57

5 **T4.4** Listen and circle the symbol that matches the sound of the underlined letters.

1 b<u>u</u>s   /ʊ/ /ʌ/   6 sh<u>o</u>p   /ʌ/ /ɒ/
2 t<u>a</u>ll   /ɑː/ /ɔː/   7 <u>a</u>pples   /æ/ /ə/
3 w<u>o</u>rd   /ɜː/ /ɔː/   8 bl<u>ue</u>   /ʊ/ /uː/
4 g<u>oo</u>d   /ʊ/ /ɔː/   9 cigar<u>e</u>tte /ʌ/ /ə/
5 p<u>a</u>rk   /æ/ /ɑː/

▶▶ p57

6 These words are written in phonemic symbols. Transcribe them.

1 /blæk/ _____
2 /ˈbʌtə/ _____
3 /pɒt/ _____
4 /klʌb/ _____
5 /egz/ _____

6 /skuːl/ _____
7 /gɜːl/ _____
8 /stɔːz/ _____
9 /kɑː/ _____
10 /kiː/ _____

►► p57

7 Turn to the Sound symbol chart on p55. Write in example words to help you remember the single vowel symbols. Underline the letters that match the sound symbols.

Word focus

Containers

1 Look at the different kinds of container.

1 bottle _____ , _____

2 packet _____ , _____

3 box _____ , _____

4 tin _____ , _____

5 can _____ , _____

6 jar _____ , _____

7 tube _____ , _____

8 carton _____ , _____

Match each pair of things with a container.

sardines/tomatoes	eggs/juice
matches/chocolates	cola/beer
toothpaste/glue	coffee/jam
wine/lemonade	sugar/crisps

►► p57

2 **T4.5** Listen and correct the mistakes in this shopping list.

6 cans of ~~cola~~ beer
a couple of cartons of eggs
2 bottles of wine (1 red, 1 rosé)
2 packets of crisps (barbecue flavour)
a tin of green olives
a small jar of coffee
a box of safety matches
a big tube of glue

►► p57

We don't stress the word *of* in fast speech. We pronounce it /əv/ and we always link it to the final consonant sound of the word before:
/lə v/
a bottle of wine

3 **T4.6** Listen to the correct items on the list and repeat them.

Intonation and sentence stress

List intonation

1 Work out the anagrams of these clothes words.

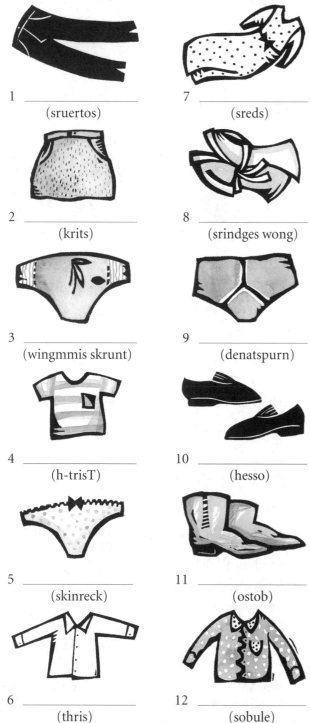

1 _____
(sruertos)

2 _____
(krits)

3 _____
(wingmmis skrunt)

4 _____
(h-trisT)

5 _____
(skinreck)

6 _____
(thris)

7 _____
(sreds)

8 _____
(srindges wong)

9 _____
(denatspurn)

10 _____
(hesso)

11 _____
(ostob)

12 _____
(sobule)

13 _____
(sampjay)

15 _____
(eti)

14 _____
(arb)

T4.7 Listen and check your answers.

▶▶ p58

Listen again and repeat the words, paying attention to the pronunciation.

2 **T4.8** Listen to this list of clothes. Which intonation pattern do you hear?

1 I bought a shirt, a tie, and some trousers.

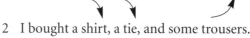

2 I bought a shirt, a tie, and some trousers.

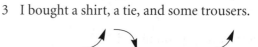

3 I bought a shirt, a tie, and some trousers.

4 I bought a shirt, a tie, and some trousers.

▶▶ p58

3 **T4.9** Listen to some people playing the game 'My sister Sally went to the summer sales …'.

Play the game in groups of four. Don't write anything. Listen to the person who speaks before you. Remember the clothes and colours he/she says, and add something. (Sally can buy things for her boyfriend, Sam, too!)

Rules of the game
- If you forget something, you are out of the game.
- The last person in the game is the winner.

Pay attention to your intonation as you play.

▶▶ p58

5

The sound /w/
Rhythm and /ə/
Hearing the difference between polite and impolite offers

Sounds

The sound /w/

1 Circle the words in the box which contain a /w/ sound.

warm	how	heavy	violence
leaving	world	when	watch
two	languages	borrow	favourite
own	views	worried	questions

T5.1 Listen and check your answers. You will only hear the words with a /w/ sound.

▶▶ p58

2 **T5.2** Listen to some students saying these sentences. Mark the pronunciation of the /w/ words right (✓) or wrong (✗).

1 Can I have some *wine*?

2 *Would* you like anything to drink?

3 He *won't* talk to his mother.

4 It's in the *west* of Hungary.

5 You need to buy a new *wheel*.

6 It's the *worst* film I've ever seen.

> To make the sound /w/, first practise /uː/. Push your lips out, and make them round and hard. /w/ is a short sound.
>
> /w/
>
> If saying /w/ at the beginning of words is difficult for you, put a word that ends with a rounded vowel or diphthong sound (*two, saw, no, now*) in front of the /w/ word.

▶▶ p58

3 **T5.3** Listen and practise.

two
two wallets
I found   two wallets.

4 Say these sentences in the same way. Start with the word before the /w/ word each time.

1 They saw wild koalas in the trees.

2 There's no wine in the shop.

3 Now wait a minute!

4 She bought him a new watch.

5 Match the questions with the answers.

1 Where was Wendy while they were watching the whales?	a The sweet white one, Walter.
2 What was wrong with the weather on Wednesday?	b Working in Washington.
3 Which wine would you like, Winifred?	c They didn't want Will to worry.
4 Why were Wayne and Wanda whispering?	d It was wet and windy.

T5.4 Listen and check your answers.

▶▶ p58

6 Work with a partner. Practise the questions and answers.

Sentence stress

Rhythm and /ə/

1 Some syllables are 'heavier' than others in the following poem. We stress them because they are in important words.

T5.5 Listen and mark the stresses ●. The first verse and the last verse are done for you.

FUTURE INTENTIONS

In June this year I'll finish school,

And the summer's getting near.

My classmates all know what they want to do,

But I haven't got any idea.

5 Pippa's going to travel round the world.

Hannah's going to stay at home.

Peter's going to join a punk rock band,

And Richard's going to teach in Rome.

Amanda's going to move to Hollywood

10 Where she hopes to become a star.

Frank's going to pass his driving test,

And then he's going to buy himself a car.

Paula's going to study up at Cambridge,

And Roger's going to learn how to cook.

15 Emma's going to have a lot of babies,

And Sarah's going to write a book.

Steven's going to be a scientist

And try to help the human race.

Helen's going to be in the Olympic team,

20 And finish in the long jump in first place.

Ian's going to be a millionaire,

And Anna's going to help the poor.

But I still don't know what I want to do,

So I'll sit here and I'll think some more.

▶▶ p58

2 How many syllables (stressed and unstressed) are there in the eight lines below? (*going* counts as one syllable in fast speech.)

line 3   My classmates all know what they want to do
  ☐ *syllables*

line 6   Hannah's going to stay at home
  ☐ *syllables*

line 7   Peter's going to join a punk rock band
  ☐ *syllables*

line 8   And Richard's going to teach in Rome
  ☐ *syllables*

line 11 Frank's going to pass his driving test
  ☐ *syllables*

line 12 And then he's going to buy himself a car
  ☐ *syllables*

line 14 And Roger's going to learn how to cook
  ☐ *syllables*

line 19 Helen's going to be in the Olympic team
  ☐ *syllables*

►► p59

3 The unstressed syllables are 'squashed' between the stresses. Very often the sound in these unstressed syllables is /ə/.

T5.6 Listen to these words and names. Notice the unstressed /ə/ sounds.

/ə/ ● /ə/   ●   /ə/   /ə/●   ● /ə/   ● /ə/
Amanda   summer   Olympics   human   Anna

4 **T5.7** Listen to the eight lines below. Mark the /ə/ sounds in each line.

                                                    /ə/
line 3   My classmates all know what they want to do

              /ə/ /ə/ /ə/   /ə/
line 6   Hannah's going to stay at home

line 7   Peter's going to join a punk rock band

line 8   And Richard's going to teach in Rome

line 11 Frank's going to pass his driving test

line 12 And then he's going to buy himself a car

line 14 And Roger's going to learn how to cook

line 19 Helen's going to be in the Olympic team

►► p59

Now listen again and repeat each line above. Follow the stress pattern you hear on the recording.

5 Work in groups of four. Choose an odd numbered line, as follows:
Student A – *line 3*   Student C – *line 11*
Student B – *line 7*   Student D – *line 19*

You're going to have a speaking race. Say your line together with the other students in your group. All start at the same time and all speak as fast as you can.

Who was the winner? Did any of you finish at the same time?

Now do the same with an even numbered line, as follows:
Student A – *line 6*   Student C – *line 12*
Student B – *line 8*   Student D – *line 14*

►► p59

6 **T5.8** Listen to the first verse of the poem with rhythm clicks. As you listen, clap with the recording.

◄ **T5.5** Listen to the whole poem again. Clap the rhythm as you read aloud with the recording.

Intonation

Hearing the difference between polite and impolite offers

1 Read the dialogues. The offers are underlined.

Excuse me, can you tell me where platform six is?

INFORMATION

Come with me. I'll show you.

Excuse me, could you tell me where the cat food is, please?

Come with me. I'll show you.

T5.9 Listen to the difference between the offers.

In Dialogue A the woman is interested and **polite**.
In Dialogue B the woman is uninterested and **impolite**.

2 Read these dialogues. Underline the offers.

1 ☐ **Jane** Oh, no! My skirt looks terrible, and I'm going out in ten minutes.
Paul I'll iron it for you.

2 ☐ **Rob** I'd like to have a look at that red coat.
Assistant I'll get it for you in a moment. I'm busy right now.

3 ☐ **Boss** I told you yesterday that there weren't any stamps.
Secretary I'm sorry, I forgot. I'll buy some now.

4 ☐ **Duncan** I couldn't do the maths homework last night. Could you?
Nick It was easy. I'll do it for you.

5 ☐ **Driver** The red light's on and it's making a terrible noise. Can you do something about it quickly?
Mechanic OK. I'll have a look at the engine for you.

▶▶ p59

3 **T5.10** Listen and mark the offers **Polite** (**P**) or **Impolite** (**I**) in the box on the left in 2.

▶▶ p59

- To sound polite in English, it is important to change the 'music' of your voice.

- To make a polite offer your intonation should go up on the stressed word, fall, then go up a little at the end. The higher up you go at the start, the more polite you sound.

■↘↗

T5.11 I'll show it to you.

4 **T5.12** Listen and practise.

I'll buy it for you.
I'll clean them for you.
I'll carry it for you.
I'll get some for you.

5 Complete each dialogue with an offer from 4.

1 **A** Oh dear. I forgot to buy any eggs.
B _____

2 **A** This suitcase is so heavy, I can't possibly carry it up those stairs.
B _____

3 **A** I can't serve drinks in these dirty glasses.
B _____

4 **A** I'm not having lunch today because I left my purse at home.
B _____

▶▶ p59

6 **T5.13** Now practise making the offers politely.

Oh dear. I forgot to buy any eggs.
You hear

I'll get some for you.
You say

I'll get some for you.
You hear

6

The sounds /n/ and /ŋ/ (and /ŋg/ and /ndʒ/)
Three-syllable nouns
Hearing different forms of *like*

Sounds

The sounds /n/ and /ŋ/ (and /ŋg/ and /ndʒ/)

1 **T6.1** Listen to these words. The **A** words end in the sound /n/. The **B** words end in the sound /ŋ/. Can you hear the difference?

A   thin   win

B   thing   wing

2 The letter *n* is sometimes pronounced /n/ and sometimes /ŋ/. Put the words in the box into the correct column below.

winter	modern	drink	window
sink	think	ankle	bank
junk	thanks	children	uncle
friendly	pond	newsagent	expensive

/n/	/ŋ/
winter	sink

T6.2 Listen and check your answers.

►► p59

3 Complete the rule.

> The letter *n* is pronounced /ŋ/ when the following sound is /_____/.

►► p59

- To make the sound /n/, put your tongue forward and up to touch the top of your mouth. Open your lips, and push air out through your nose. /n/ is a voiced sound.

- To make the sound /ŋ/, put your tongue in the position to make the sound /k/. Keeping your tongue in that position, try to say /n/. /ŋ/ is a voiced sound.

4 Listen again to the /n/ and /ŋ/ words in 2 and practise saying them.

T6.3 The letters *ng* can be pronounced /ŋ/, /ŋg/ or /ndʒ/. Listen.

/ŋ/ thing   /ŋg/ hungry   /ndʒ/ danger

5 Put these words into the columns below.

singing	strange	wrong	congratulations
stronger	young	oranges	exchanged
wedding	single	bungalow	buildings
English	darling	changing	king

/ŋ/	/ŋg/	/ndʒ/
thing	**hungry**	**danger**

T6.4 Listen and check your answers.

▶▶ p59

6 Complete the rule.

> The letters *ng* at the end of a word are always
> pronounced /_____/.

▶▶ p59

7 **T6.5** Listen to some students saying these sentences.
Circle where they make mistakes with the sound /ŋ/.

1 He's stronger than Hercules.

2 Can't you see anything?

3 Are you enjoying it here?

4 I'll ring up later.

5 He goes jogging every day.

6 My brother often goes fishing.

▶▶ p59

8 Match up these mini-dialogues.

1 Captain! I think
   we're sinking.

   a All right, Angela, you
   can exchange it for
   another one.

2 Have you got an
   English–Hungarian
   dictionary?

   b But darling, he's
   single, ninety-nine,
   and his only niece
   lives in Montreal.

3 This orange looks
   strange, miss.

   c Incredible! They said
   the *Titanic* was
   unsinkable.

4 We're not inviting
   that boring old thing
   for Christmas!

   d Bilingual dictionaries
   are with the foreign
   language books on the
   second floor, sir.

T6.6 Listen and check your answers.

▶▶ p59

9 Work with a partner. Practise the dialogues containing
sounds which are a problem for you.

Word focus

Three-syllable words

1 **T6.7** Listen and say these names with the correct stress.

Melanie   Rebecca   Bernadette

2 What are Melanie, Rebecca, and Bernadette like?

3 **T6.8** Listen and write these words in the correct part of the table below, according to meaning and stress.

good-looking	romantic	tomatoes
overweight	unemployed	carrot soup
beautiful	journalist	Aberdeen
sociable	musician	Birmingham
impolite	sausages	Bologna

	● ● ● **Melanie**	● ● ● **Rebecca**	● ● ● **Bernadette**
looks			
character			
job			
favourite food			
favourite city			

4 **T6.9** Listen and check your answers. Who do you think is the best girlfriend for Luigi?

> **Luigi – Italian, attractive, old-fashioned, artistic – is seeking a girlfriend.**

▶▶ p60

Listen again and practise saying the words with the correct stress.

> The main stress in ● ● ● words changes when they are followed by stressed nouns.
>
>   ●
>
> He's a little overweight.
>
>   ●   ●
>
> He's an overweight politician.

5 **T6.10** Listen to these sentences and mark the main stress on the underlined words.

1 She's a <u>magazine</u> journalist.

2 We waited in the airport for <u>seventeen</u> hours.

3 Who wants to be a <u>millionaire</u>?

4 We've got a <u>second-hand</u> car.

5 Todd's only <u>seventeen</u>.

6 Mr Green was a <u>millionaire</u> businessman.

7 *Arena*'s my favourite <u>magazine</u>.

8 I bought my computer <u>second hand</u>.

▶▶ p60

Connected speech

Hearing different forms of *like*

1 **T6.11** Listen and tick (✓) the sentences you hear.

1   a   What's your sister like?
    b   What does your sister like?   ✓

2   a   I'd like a strawberry ice-cream.
    b   I like strawberry ice-cream.

3   a   Would you like to go dancing?
    b   Do you like going dancing?

4   a   Tina's like her mother.
    b   Tina likes her mother.

5   a   How do you like your coffee?
    b   How would you like your coffee?

6   a   We aren't like each other.
    b   We don't like each other.

▶▶ p60

2 **T6.12** Listen and complete the sentences below.

1 She <u>'s very like</u> her mother.

2 He _____ his elder sister.

3 I _____ in London.

4 What _____ drink?

5 He _____ anyone in his family.

6 _____ like you?

▶▶ p60

7

Consonant symbols 2
The sounds /θ/ and /ð/
Present Perfect and Past Simple

Sound symbols

Consonant symbols 2

1 **T7.1** Listen to these sound symbols and example words. Memorize the sound of each symbol.

/ʃ/ Engli<u>sh</u>, _____ , _____

/ʒ/ televi<u>s</u>ion, _____ , _____

/t/ + /ʃ/ = /tʃ/ wat<u>ch</u>, _____ , _____

/d/ + /ʒ/ = /dʒ/ colle<u>g</u>e, _____ , _____

/θ/ <u>th</u>irties, _____ , _____

/ð/ <u>th</u>en, _____ , _____

/j/ <u>y</u>es, _____ , _____

/ŋ/ si<u>ng</u>er, _____ , _____

2 **T7.2** Listen to these words. Write two of them next to each sound symbol above, according to the sound of the underlined letters.

<u>s</u>ugar	sou<u>th</u>	<u>y</u>ou	<u>th</u>is
mat<u>ch</u>es	chan<u>g</u>ed	bir<u>th</u>day	lon<u>g</u>
u<u>s</u>ually	spe<u>c</u>ial	dru<u>n</u>k	<u>Eu</u>rope
toge<u>th</u>er	<u>j</u>ust	plea<u>s</u>ure	<u>ch</u>eap

▶▶ p60

3 Write as many crazy example sentences as you can with the groups of three words. Practise saying them.

THIS IS SPECIAL ENGLISH SUGAR!

Look at the groups of symbols below.
A contains voiceless sounds.
B contains voiced sounds.

SHHHH!

A
/ʃ/ /tʃ/ /θ/

YEAH!

B
/ʒ/ /dʒ/ /ð/ /j/ /ŋ/

4 **T7.3** Listen and repeat the sounds.

5 **T7.4** Listen to these words and circle the correct phonetic transcription.

1 jeans
   a /dʒiːnz/
   b /jiːnz/
   c /jiːns/

2 shepherd
   a /ˈtʃepherd/
   b /ˈshefəd/
   c /ˈʃepəd/

3 chef
   a /shef/
   b /ʃef/
   c /tʃef/

4 Thursday
   a /ˈtʃɜːrzdeɪ/
   b /ˈthʊrsdɑːj/
   c /ˈθɜːzdeɪ/

5 watch
   a /wɒtʃ/
   b /wɒtsh/
   c /wɑːθ/

6 measure
   a /ˈmeɑːʃə/
   b /ˈmeʒuːre/
   c /ˈmeʒə/

7 hungry
   a /ˈhʌngri/
   b /ˈhʌŋri/
   c /ˈhʌŋgri/

8 father
   a /ˈfɑːther/
   b /ˈfɑːðə/
   c /ˈfɑːðer/

▶▶ p60

6 Turn to the Sound symbol chart on p55. Write example words to help you remember the consonant symbols you have just learnt. Underline the letters that match the sound symbols.

Sounds

The sounds /θ/ and /ð/

1 The letters *th* can be pronounced /θ/ or /ð/. Put these words into the columns below, according to the pronunciation of the letters *th*.

grandfather	other	them	three
north	things	clothes	athlete
health	months	their	leather

/θ/	/ð/
north	grandfather

T7.5 Listen and check your answers.

▶▶ p60

2 Can you add more words to the columns above?

- To make the sound /θ/, touch the back of your top teeth with your tongue. Push out air between your teeth and your tongue. /θ/ is a voiceless sound.

- To make the sound /ð/, make the sound /θ/ but use your voice.

- If you have problems making the sounds /θ/ and /ð/, put your finger in front of your mouth and touch it with your tongue, like this:

- Learners of English sometimes pronounce the sound /θ/ as /s/, /t/, or /f/.

- Learners of English sometimes pronounce the sound /ð/ as /z/, /d/, or /v/.

3 **T7.6** Listen to some students reading these mini-dialogues aloud. Circle the *th* sounds which they pronounce incorrectly.

A Sorry I broke (those) plates.

B That's all right. I didn't really like them.

C There are your theatre tickets!

D Thanks a lot.

E It's Tom's birthday on Thursday.

F Yes, and I haven't got him anything.

G Do you like my leather trousers?

H I think they're great!

I How much is that watch worth?

J About thirty pounds.

K This music's boring.

L Shh! My brother likes the Beatles!

►► p60

4 Read the mini-dialogues aloud with a partner. Pronounce the letters *th* correctly.

Connected speech

Present Perfect and Past Simple – the pronunciation of 's

1 **T7.7** Look at these pairs of sentences. Listen and tick (✓) the sentences you hear.

1 a Philip bought you a lovely present.
   b Philip's bought you a lovely present. ✓

2 a I never liked maths.
   b I've never liked maths.

3 a She never invited me to her flat.
   b She's never invited me to her flat.

4 a Who burnt the frying-pan?
   b Who's burnt the frying-pan?

5 a Nick posted that letter.
   b Nick's posted that letter.

6 a Tell me what happened!
   b Tell me what's happened!

7 a We lived in London for two years.
   b We've lived in London for two years.

▶▶ p60

> You can hear the 's more easily when the following word starts with a vowel sound.

2 **T7.8** Listen to these sentences. When do you pronounce 's as /s/? When do you pronounce 's as /z/?

1 She's answered my letter.
2 Who's unlocked the desk drawer?
3 It's arrived!
4 Inspector Brown's examined the room.
5 Jack's entered the disco dancing competition.
6 My wife's invited her mother to stay.
7 David's ordered some champagne.
8 That new record shop's opened.

▶▶ p60

3 Look back at the Present Perfect sentences in 1. In which sentences should you pronounce 's as /s/? In which sentences should you pronounce 's as /z/?

▶▶ p60

4 Read the sentences in 1 and 2 aloud. Pay attention to the pronunciation of 's.

8

The sounds /ʃ/, /s/, and /tʃ/
The sounds /ʊ/ and /u:/
Questions with *or*

Sounds

The sounds /ʃ/, /s/, and /tʃ/

1 **T8.1** Listen to the dialogue.

OH, SHIRLEY! THE INK ON SHANE'S SHORTS JUST WON'T WASH OUT.

SHOUT

YOU SHOULD USE 'SHOUT'—THE PRE-WASH CLEANER, SHEILA.

> We nearly always pronounce the letters *sh* as /ʃ/. We can write the sound /ʃ/ in other ways too.

2 **T8.2** Listen. In one word in each line below, the underlined letters are pronounced /ʃ/. Circle those words.

1 <u>ch</u>ef	<u>ch</u>ildren	me<u>ch</u>anic	tea<u>ch</u>er
2 <u>c</u>igarette	ex<u>c</u>iting	spe<u>c</u>ial	<u>c</u>ity
3 <u>s</u>uccessful	mea<u>s</u>ure	<u>s</u>un	<u>s</u>ure
4 profe<u>ss</u>ion	<u>s</u>ight	televi<u>s</u>ion	<u>s</u>ingle
5 re<u>t</u>ired	recep<u>t</u>ionist	ar<u>t</u>ist	fantas<u>t</u>ic
6 ne<u>c</u>essary	ex<u>c</u>ellent	<u>c</u>ertain	o<u>c</u>ean

▶▶ p60

 The sound /ʃ/ is often confused with /s/ and /tʃ/.

3 **T8.3** Listen. Circle the words you hear twice.

1	ship	chip
2	she	sea
3	shoes	choose
4	short	sort
5	cash	catch
6	show	sew
7	washing	watching
8	sheet	seat

▶▶ p60

4 Practise the sounds. Do not use your voice.

- To make the sound /s/, your tongue should be forward. /s/ is the sound that starts the word *sip*. It can be long. (Think of a snake!)

- To make the sound /ʃ/, first practise /s/. Now move your tongue back and up a little. /ʃ/ is the sound that starts the word *ship*. It can be long. (Think of someone saying 'Be quiet'!)

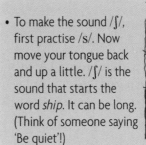

- To make the sound /tʃ/, first practise /t/ and /ʃ/. Begin to make /t/. Now move your tongue away from the top of your mouth. /tʃ/ is the sound that starts the word *chip*. It is always short.

5 Work on your own. Write down ten words from 3.

6 Work with a partner. Dictate your ten words to your partner. Write down the ten words he/she dictates to you. When you have finished, compare your lists of words.

7 Read these headlines. Count the /ʃ/ sounds in each sentence.

> **English Shoppers Short of Cash**
>
> **Swedish Fashion Show Shocks British**
>
> *Inflation Hits Russian Champagne*
>
> **Ambitious Scottish Receptionist Shoots Boss**
>
> *Irish Fishing Ship Sinks in Pacific Ocean*

▶▶ p61

T8.4 Listen and practise saying the headlines.

The sounds /ʊ/ and /uː/

1 Work with a partner. Use a dictionary if you need to. Make sure you understand all the words in the boxes below.

Box S	Box L
full	fool
pull	pool
look	Luke
soot	suit

2 **T8.5** You will hear eight pairs of words. Listen and decide. Are the words in each pair the same or different?

Example

1 (full ... full)

1	(same)	different	5	same	different
2	same	different	6	same	different
3	same	different	7	same	different
4	same	different	8	same	different

▶▶ p61

- In the words in **Box S**, the vowel sound is /ʊ/. It is a short sound.

- In the words in **Box L**, the vowel sound is /uː/. It is a long sound.

3 Practise making the sounds.

- To make the sound /ʊ/, open your lips a little and make them a little round. Keep the sound short.

/ʊ/

- To make the sound /uː/, make your lips very round and hard. Make the sound long.

/uː/

4 **T8.6** Listen and circle the words you hear in these sentences.

1 How do you spell '*full*' / '*fool*'?

2 It says '*Pull*' / '*Pool*' on that door.

3 *Look* / *Luke*, will you be quiet?

4 Don't leave that *soot* / *suit* there!

▶▶ p61

5 Look up the meaning of these words in a dictionary.

a room with a view	a look at the woods
an afternoon cruise	fondues or barbecues
Would you like new boots?	book through Thomas Cook
a few queues	good food
fruit with sugar	I shouldn't be rude
a shoe museum	You couldn't do better

6 **T8.7** Listen and mark the /ʊ/, /uː/, and /juː/ sounds as follows:

Circle the /ʊ/ sounds like this: rom

Underline the /uː/ and /juː/ sounds like this: view.

▶▶ p61

7 Practise saying the words, paying attention to the long and short *u* sounds.

Intonation and sentence stress

Questions with *or*

1 **T8.8** We ask *or* questions when we give someone a choice of two things. Listen to this question with *or*. Which intonation pattern do you hear?

1 Do you want tea or coffee?

2 Do you want tea or coffee?

3 Do you want tea or coffee?

4 Do you want tea or coffee?

▶▶ p61

2 Lord and Lady Sneer are formal, but unfriendly.

James and Bridget are informal, but friendly.

T8.9 You will hear three dialogues. Listen and decide. Are the people formal or informal? Are they friendly or unfriendly?

▶▶ p61

3 Listen again and complete the dialogues.

1 **A** Do you want __tea__ or __coffee__ ?

   B Oh, _____ , please.

   A _____ or _____ ?

   B _____ , please.

   A With _____ or without?

   B Oh, no _____ for me, please.

2 **C** Would you like _____ or _____ with the meal?

   D Mmm … I think _____ would be nice.

   C All right. Would you prefer _____ or _____ ?

   D Erm … _____ , I think.

3 **E** Next, please. Can I help you?

   F A _____ and a _____ , please.

   E _____ or _____ ?

   F _____ , please.

   E To _____ _____ or _____ _____ ?

   F _____ _____ , please.

▶▶ p61

4 Work with a partner. Read each dialogue aloud. Pay attention to your intonation.

5 Now choose one dialogue and read it twice. The first time make your voices flat and hard. Be unfriendly! The second time make your voices soft. Be friendly.

6 Act out your dialogue in front of the class. Everyone has to guess – are you being friendly or unfriendly?

9 The sounds /iː/ and /ɪ/
Word counting and sentence stress patterns
Showing interest and surprise

Sounds

The sounds /iː/ and /ɪ/

1 Work with a partner. Use a dictionary if you need to. Make sure you understand all the words in the boxes.

Do these fit your feet?

	Box L	Box S
1	feet	fit
2	seat	sit
3	steal	still
4	feel	fill
5	jeans	gins
6	beans	bins
7	team	Tim
8	cheap	chip
9	peach	pitch
10	leave	live

2 **T9.1** Listen to the recording. Circle the words you hear.

▶▶ p61

- In the words in **Box L**, the vowel sound is /iː/.
- In the words in **Box S**, the vowel sound is /ɪ/.

3 Practise making the sounds.

- To make the sound /iː/, smile and open your mouth a little. /iː/ is a long sound. It comes in the words *feet* and *seat*.

- To make the sound /ɪ/, open your mouth a little more. /ɪ/ is a short sound. It comes in the words *fit* and *sit*.

4 **T9.2** Listen to the recording and write the words you hear in the gaps in the sentences below.

1 Those are large __*gins*__ !
2 Can you _____ that?
3 Has your _____ lost the match?
4 Those are nice _____.
5 How are you going to _____?
6 What a hard _____!

Check your answers with a partner.

▶▶ p61

5 Look at these words with a partner. Box ☐ the /i:/ words and circle ◯ the /ɪ/ words according to the sound of the underlined letters. Use a dictionary if you don't know the meaning or pronunciation of the words.

w<u>ee</u>k	<u>e</u>nough	r<u>e</u>member	tr<u>i</u>p
b<u>u</u>siness	m<u>e</u>	bic<u>y</u>cles	p<u>eo</u>ple
fin<u>i</u>shed	mess<u>a</u>ge	v<u>i</u>sa	s<u>ea</u>son

T9.3 Listen and check your answers.

▶▶ p61

6 Listen again and practise saying the words with the recording.

7 Work on your own. Write down ten words from the boxes in 1.

Seat

8 Work with a partner. Dictate your ten words to your partner. Write down the ten words he/she dictates to you. When you have finished, compare your lists of words.

Connected speech

Word counting and sentence stress patterns

1 **T9.4** Listen. How many words do you hear in each sentence? Contractions count as two words.

Example

     1 2 3   4 5 6   7 8   9 10 11

Where'll you go if you don't find a hotel? = 11 words

1 **8** _____

_____ .

2 ☐ _____

_____ ?

3 ☐ _____

_____ .

4 ☐ _____

_____ .

5 ☐ _____

_____ ?

6 ☐ _____

_____ ?

7 ☐ _____

_____ .

8 ☐ _____

_____ .

▶▶ p61

2 Listen again. Write the sentences you hear in the gaps in 1.

▶▶ p61

3 Look at the stress patterns for sentences 1, 2, and 3. Listen to them again. Notice the sentence stress and contracted forms.

1 ● ● ● ● ● ● ● ●
2 ● ● ● ● ● ● ● ● ●
3 ● ● ● ● ● ●

4 Now look at the stress patterns for sentences 4–8. Listen again and count the syllables. Which stress pattern matches which sentence? Write the number of the sentence.

a ● ● ● ● ● ● ☐
b ● ● ● ● ● ● ● ● ☐
c ● ● ● ● ● ● ☐
d ● ● ● ● ● ● ☐
e ● ● ● ● ● ☐

▶▶ p61

5 Listen again and repeat the sentences. Make sure you put the stress in the correct places, and don't forget the contracted forms.

Intonation and sentence stress

Showing interest and surprise

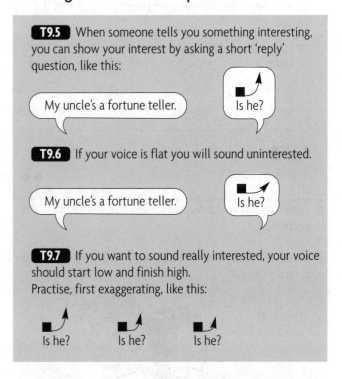

T9.5 When someone tells you something interesting, you can show your interest by asking a short 'reply' question, like this:

My uncle's a fortune teller. / Is he?

T9.6 If your voice is flat you will sound uninterested.

My uncle's a fortune teller. / Is he?

T9.7 If you want to sound really interested, your voice should start low and finish high.
Practise, first exaggerating, like this:

Is he? Is he? Is he?

1 Look at the rules for making reply questions.

Rules

- When the verb *be* is in the sentence, use the correct form of *be* in the reply question.

  My uncle's a fortune teller.
  Is he?

- When another auxiliary verb is in the sentence, use the correct form of that verb in the reply question.

  He's got a gypsy caravan.
  Has he?

- When there is no auxiliary verb in the sentence, use the correct form of *do*.

  He likes looking into the future.
  Does he?

2 Complete this conversation with reply questions.

My aunt's a fortune teller.

1 _____ ?

Yeah, she uses a crystal ball to see into the future.

2 _____ ?

Mmm. It belonged to my granny.

3 _____ ?

Yeah. She can read the lines on your hand as well.

4 _____ ?

And she's also got some very old Tarot cards.

5 _____ ?

Yeah, one pack is over 100 years old.

6 _____ ?

Mmm. And she's recently bought a horoscope programme for her computer.

7 _____ ?

Oh, yes. There's a computer in her caravan, you see.

8 _____ ?

Mmm. And now I'm interested in fortune telling.

9 _____ ?

What's more I've started reading lots of books about it.

10 _____ ?

Yes. And sometimes my friends ask me to tell their fortunes.

11 _____ ?

Naturally I always say yes.

12 _____ ?

T9.8 Listen and check your answers.

▶▶ p61

3 Listen again and repeat the reply questions with the recording. Sound interested.

4 Work on your own. Write down some surprising 'facts' about a relative of yours. (You don't have to be truthful!)

Example
My wife's a film star.
She's got a house in Beverly Hills.
I'm her sixth husband.

5 **T9.9** Listen to the short dialogue below. Can you hear that **B**'s voice starts very low and goes up very high at the end of each question?

A My wife's a film star.

B Is she?

A Yes. She's got a house in Beverly Hills.

B Has she?

A Yes. Of course, I'm her sixth husband.

B Are you?

6 Now work with a partner to make similar dialogues.

Student A Tell your partner what you have written down.

Student B Show your surprise, using reply questions. Pay attention to your intonation.

When you finish, swap roles.

10

'Double vowel' or diphthong symbols
Strong form prepositions at the end of questions
Contractions

Sounds

Diphthong symbols

Diphthongs are 'double vowel sounds'.

1 Put these words into the gaps in the phrases below. Use the pictures and a dictionary to help you.

bear	beer	bow	boy
cow	fly	Grey	hair
hello	tie	tour	crow
deer	toy	way	Moor

1 a **bear** combing   3 a _____
his **hair** .   making a _____ .

2 a _____   4 a _____ holding
wearing a _____ .   a _____ .

5 a _____   7 Mr _____
drinking a   asking the

_____ .   _____ .

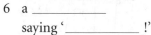

6 a _____   8 Mrs _____
saying '_____ !'   on a _____ .

T10.1 Listen and check your answers.

▶▶ p61

2 Listen again and memorize the phrases. Each phrase practises a diphthong symbol. (Can you find the symbols in the pictures?)

3 **T10.2** Listen to these sound symbols and example words. Memorize the sound of each diphthong.

/e/ + /ɪ/ = /eɪ/   day,

_____ , _____

/ɑː/ + /ɪ/ = /aɪ/   my,

_____ , _____

/ɔː/ + /ɪ/ = /ɔɪ/   boy,

_____ , _____

/ɪ/ + /ə/ = /ɪə/   near,

_____ , _____

/e/ + /ə/ = /eə/   where,

_____ , _____

/ə/ + /ʊ/ = /əʊ/   go,

_____ , _____

/ɑː/ + /ʊ/ = /aʊ/   now,

_____ , _____

/ʊ/ + /ə/ = /ʊə/   tour*

_____ , _____

* Many younger native speakers rarely use this sound. They often use /ɔː/ instead.

4 **T10.3** Listen to these words. Write them next to the diphthong symbols above, according to the sounds of the underlined letters.

bu_y_	rep_ai_r	_o_nly	h_ou_se
h_e_re	tr_ai_n	tr_y_	h_o_me
br_ow_n	enj_oy_ed	cl_ea_r	n_oi_sy
p_oo_r	w_ay_	th_e_re	s_u_re

▶▶ p61

5 **T10.4** Listen to these words and circle the correct phonetic transcription.

1 wide   a /weɪd/   b (/waɪd/)   c /wɪəd/
2 place   a /pleɪs/   b /plaɪs/   c /pleəs/
3 poison   a /ˈpɔɪzən/   b /ˈpəʊzən/   c /ˈpaʊzən/
4 hear   a /heə/   b /hʊə/   c /hɪə/
5 nowhere   a /ˈnəʊweɪ/   b /ˈnəʊweə/   c /ˈnəʊwɪə/
6 round   a /rəʊnd/   b /rɔɪnd/   c /raʊnd/
7 slowly   a /ˈsleəli/   b /ˈsləʊli/   c /ˈslaʊli/
8 Europe   a /ˈjaʊrəp/   b /ˈjeɪrəp/   c /ˈjʊərəp/

▶▶ p61

6 Turn to the Sound symbol chart on p55. Write in example words to help you remember the double vowel symbols. Underline the letters that match the sound symbols.

Connected speech

Strong form prepositions at the end of questions

1 Read part of the story 'Love on a train'. Put a word from the box into each gap.

to	about	to	at
at	off	from	in

For some time Nancy looked (1) **_at_** the handsome young man sitting opposite her.

Finally he smiled (2) _____ her and said 'Hello'.

It was a long trip and they talked (3) _____ lots of things. He came (4) _____ Toulouse, and he was interested (5) _____ photography. When he got (6) _____ the train in Toulouse, Nancy saw a book on the seat. She didn't know if it belonged (7) _____ the handsome Frenchman, but she decided to write (8) _____ the address in the front of the book.

T10.5 Listen and check your answers.

▶▶ p61

- Some prepositions have weak forms when they are not at the end of a sentence. In the text above, these prepositions are weak:

	Strong	Weak
to	/tuː/	/tə/
at	/æt/	/ət/
from	/frɒm/	/frəm/

- Some prepositions – like *off* /ɒf/, *about* /əˈbaʊt/, and *in* /ɪn/ – only have a strong form.

Many verbs are used with a preposition (eg *listen to, look at*). The preposition follows the verb, and so in questions it is at the end.

Example
She **looked at** the man opposite her.
Who did she **look at**?

2 Look at the text again. Write questions like the one in the example for the answers below.

1 Who _did he_ smile _at_ ? Her.

2 What _____ talk _____ ? Lots of things.

3 Where _____ come _____ ? Toulouse.

4 What _____ interested _____ ?
Photography.

5 Where _____ get _____ ? In Toulouse.

6 Who _____ belong _____ ?
She didn't know.

7 Which _____ write _____ ?
The one in the front of the book.

T10.6 Listen and check your answers.

▶▶ p61

> If a preposition is at the end of a question, the pronunciation is strong.

3 Listen again. Repeat the questions, paying attention to the strong form prepositions.

Connected speech

Contractions

> We use contractions in conversation but not formal speeches. We write contractions in letters to friends but not in business letters.
>
> Here are some rules for writing contractions.
>
> 1 We do not write contractions in short affirmative answers.
>   **Example**
>   A Is she Spanish?
>   B Yes, she is. (*not* Yes, she's.)
>
> 2 The only contraction we usually write with nouns (and names) is 's.
>   **Example**
>   Pablo's arrived.
>   The children have arrived. (*not* The children've arrived.)
>
> 3 The only contraction we usually write with non-personal pronouns (*What, Where, How, Who, When, Here, There, That,* etc.) is 's.
>   **Example**
>   Where's the toilet?
>   Where have you been? (*not* Where've you been?)

> 4 We do not write 's contractions with *Wh-* questions ending in the word *it.*
>   **Example**
>   What is it? (*not* What's it?)
>
> 5 The contracted form of *Am I not?* is *Aren't I?*
>   **Example**
>   Aren't I going with you?

1 Rewrite these sentences with contractions where you can. (There are four where you can't use contractions, and one with a strange contraction!)

1 You should not eat fatty foods.

   _____**You shouldn't eat fatty foods.**_____

2 She cannot speak Italian very well.

   _____

3 A You have not read it, have you?

   A _____

   B Yes, I have.

   B _____

4 There is a bus stop opposite the library.

   _____

5 Sean would like to be an astronaut.

   _____

6 I am right, am I not?

   _____

7 It will be the biggest city on earth.

   _____

8 What are your names?

   _____

9 Who is it?

   _____

10 I did not use to watch much TV as a child.

   _____

▶▶ p62

2 **T10.7** Listen to how the contractions are pronounced. Listen again and repeat the sentences.

11

The sounds /e/, /æ/, and /ʌ/
Word linking
Weak form auxiliaries and passive verbs

Sounds

The sounds /e/, /æ/, and /ʌ/

1 Work with a partner. Look at these groups of three words. Use a dictionary to check the meaning of any words you want.

beg   bag   bug

Ben   ban   bun

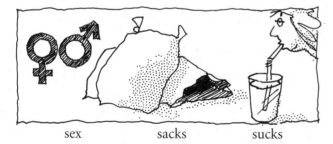

sex   sacks   sucks

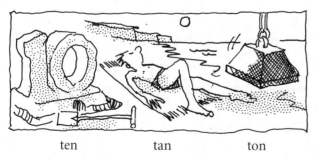

ten   tan   ton

bed   bad   bud

2 **T11.1** Listen and circle the words you hear. The first three words are circled for you. Can you hear the difference between them?

1 (beg)	bag	bug
2 bag	(bag)	bug
3 bag	bag	(bug)
4 Ben	ban	bun
5 Ben	ban	bun
6 sex	sacks	sucks
7 sex	sacks	sucks
8 ten	tan	ton
9 ten	tan	ton
10 bed	bad	bud
11 bed	bad	bud

▶▶ p62

- In the words on the left, the vowel sound is /e/.
- In the words in the middle, the vowel sound is /æ/.
- In the words on the right, the vowel sound is /ʌ/.

3 Practise saying the sounds.

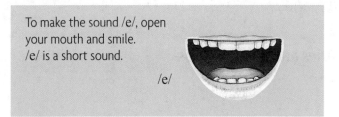

To make the sound /e/, open your mouth and smile. /e/ is a short sound.

/e/

4 `T11.2` Practise saying all the /e/ words in 1 on p41.

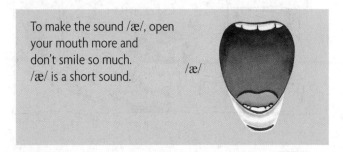

To make the sound /æ/, open your mouth more and don't smile so much. /æ/ is a short sound.

/æ/

5 `T11.3` Practise saying all the /æ/ words in 1 on p41.

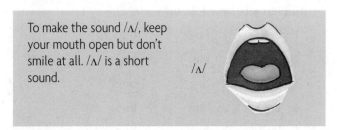

To make the sound /ʌ/, keep your mouth open but don't smile at all. /ʌ/ is a short sound.

/ʌ/

6 `T11.4` Practise saying all the /ʌ/ words in 1 on p41.

7 Work on your own. Make a list of ten words from 1.

8 Work with a partner.

Student A Say your words one by one to your partner. (Don't point or say anything but the words on your list.)

Student B Listen. After your partner says a word, point to the picture of it in 1.

Student A If your partner points to the correct picture, nod your head for 'yes'. If your partner points to the wrong picture, shake your head for 'no'.

When you have finished, swap roles. Now **B** says the words and **A** points.

9 `T11.5` Look at this map. Listen and write the numbers for the different buildings in the key below.

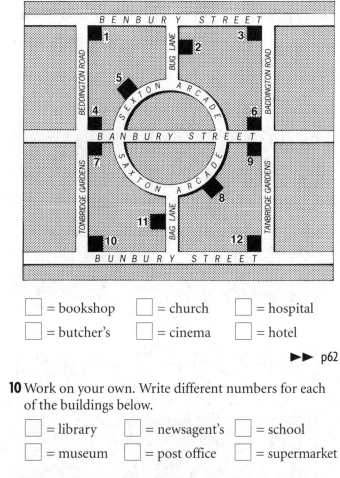

☐ = bookshop   ☐ = church   ☐ = hospital

☐ = butcher's   ☐ = cinema   ☐ = hotel

▶▶ p62

10 Work on your own. Write different numbers for each of the buildings below.

☐ = library   ☐ = newsagent's   ☐ = school

☐ = museum   ☐ = post office   ☐ = supermarket

11 Work with a partner. One of you is Student A and one of you is Student B.

Student A Ask Student B where each building is in his/her town.

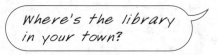

Where's the library in your town?

Student B Tell Student A where each building is in your town. (Don't point to your map!)

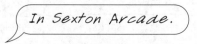

In Sexton Arcade.

When you finish, check that Student A has got the correct numbers for each building.

Now swap roles.

Student B Ask Student A where each building is in his/her town.

Student A Reply.

Connected speech

Word linking

- **T11.6** When a word begins with a vowel sound, the consonant sound at the end of the word before links on to it. (See Unit 1.)

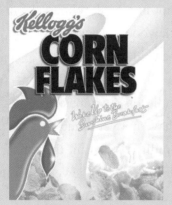

Kellogg's Corn Flakes were⌣invented⌣in⌣eighteen ninety-four.

Nike trainers⌣are sold⌣all⌣over the world.

- **T11.7** There is no linking between words when there is a pause – marked by a comma or full stop.

Ball-point pens,⌣or 'biros', were⌣invented by László Biro, a Hungarian journalist,⌣in nineteen thirty-⌣eight.

1 **T11.8** Look at the text. Listen and mark the word linking.

Most people's picture⌣of⌣a typical⌣Englishman⌣is⌣a man⌣in⌣a suit, with an umbrella, a copy of *The Times*, and a *bowler* hat. Not everyone knows, however, that this hard, low, round-brimmed hat was invented in the nineteenth century, or that it was named after a pair of British hat makers, Thomas and William Bowler.

The first example of a bowler hat was ordered by a country gentleman, Thomas Coke, who lived in Norfolk. He wanted a strong and practical hat that he could wear when he went out shooting.

In America the bowler hat is known as a *derby*.

►► p62

2 **T11.9** Listen and practise the first linked phrase, starting from the end, like this:

suit

n⌣a⌣suit

n⌣in⌣a suit

man⌣in⌣a suit, *etc.*

3 Now practise some of the other linked phrases in the passage in the same way, starting from the end each time.

4 When you are ready, try reading the whole passage aloud, paying attention to the word linking.

Weak form auxiliaries and passive verbs

1 Use a dictionary to check the meaning of the words in the box.

safe (noun)	jewels (noun)
steal (verb)	masked (adjective)
crime (noun)	robbery (noun)
shoot (verb)	reward (noun)

2 The words in 1 come from a newspaper article you are going to read. What do you think it's about?

3 **T11.10** Thirteen words are missing from the article. Listen to the complete text and put a ⟨ where there is a missing word.

BANK ROBBERY IN CRICKLEWOOD

A cleaning woman, Mrs Ethel Boggis, ⟨ shot in a bank robbery in Cricklewood yesterday evening. She said to be safe and comfortable in hospital. The bank broken into by two masked men. They have not yet found. A _____

Mrs Boggis

total of £1 million stolen in the robbery, and a bag of jewels also taken. The jewels kept in a bank safe by Lady Agatha Crickle who told the bad news late last night by the bank manager.

'Most of my jewels made of gold,' she told reporters. 'My favourite ring made in China three hundred years ago. I can't possibly buy another one.'

Lady Crickle

A red Ford Ka seen near the bank and later found in a car park at Heathrow Airport. A reward is offered by the police for any information about the crime.

4 Write in the missing words. Don't listen to the recording again.

When you finish, listen again and check your answers.

▶▶ p62

Nearly all the verbs in the passage are in the passive. Listen and notice the pronunciation of the verb *be* in the passive verb forms. It is very weak.

5 Cover the article. Work with a partner. Use the words in 1 to retell the story. Pay attention to your pronunciation of the passive verb forms.

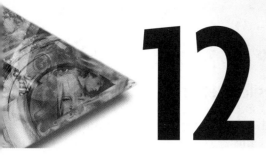

12

The sounds /e/ and /eɪ/
Words with silent letters
Linking in phrasal verbs

Sounds

The sounds /e/ and /eɪ/

1 Work with a partner. Use a dictionary if you need to. Make sure you understand all the words in the boxes below.

	Box S	Box D
1	sell	sail
2	pen	pain
3	shed	shade
4	tell	tail
5	letter	later
6	pepper	paper
7	well	whale
8	test	taste
9	wet	wait
10	get	gate

2 **T12.1** Listen and circle the words you hear twice.

►► p63

- In **Box S** the vowel sound of the underlined letters is /e/. It is a single vowel.
- In **Box D** the vowel sound of the underlined letters is /eɪ/. It is a 'double vowel sound', or diphthong, made of the sound /e/ followed by the sound /ɪ/.

3 Practise the sounds.

- To make the sound /e/, open your mouth a little and smile. /e/ is a short sound.
- To make the sound /eɪ/, first write the symbols /e/ and /ɪ/ on separate cards. Hold up the /e/ card in your left hand. Turn your head left and say /e/. Make it short. Open your mouth a little more. Turn your head right and say /ɪ/. Make it short.

T12.2 Hold up both cards. Turn your head quickly from side to side. Say /e/ when you turn left and /ɪ/ when you turn right. Keep the sounds short. Repeat this three times.

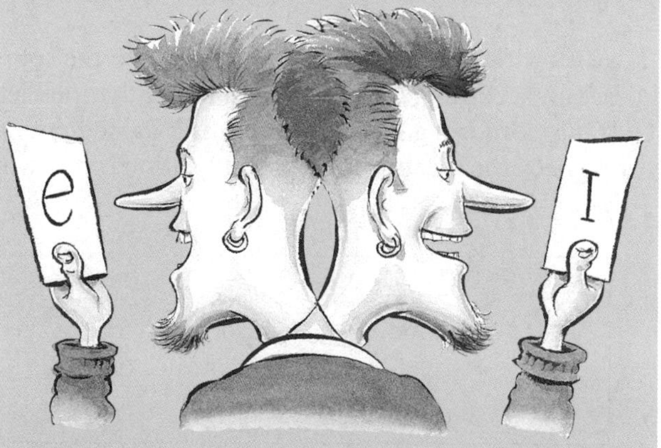

T12.3 Now turn your head left and say /e/. Make it long. Turn your head slowly right and change the /e/ sound to /ɪ/. Repeat this three times.

Now say /eɪ/ at normal speed. Remember that a diphthong is a bit longer than a single vowel sound. (Make the /e/ long and keep the /ɪ/ short!)

4 **T12.4** You will hear six questions. Tick (✓) the correct response for each question you hear.

1 Are you going to *sell* / *sail* that boat?
   a Yes, I want to buy a new one.
   b Yes, if the weather stays good.

2 Have you got a *pen* / *pain*?
   a No, but I've got a pencil.
   b Yes, in my ankle.

3 Did you want some *pepper* / *paper*?
   a No, some salt.
   b No, some card.

4 Can I see her *letter* / *later*?
   a No, it's personal.
   b Yes, I think she's free this afternoon.

5 Can you *test* / *taste* it?
   a Yes, we'll send it to the laboratory tomorrow.
   b Yes, I'm sure it's got rum in it.

6 Do you like the *shed* / *shade*?
   a Yes. Did you really make it?
   b Yes. It's too hot in the sun today.

Work with a partner. Compare your answers.

▶▶ p63

5 Work with a partner. Put these words into the columns below, according to the sound of the underlined letters. (One word can go in both columns.) Use a dictionary to check the meaning and pronunciation of the words if you want.

c<u>a</u>ke	d<u>a</u>nger	st<u>ea</u>k	ag<u>ai</u>n
l<u>e</u>t	s<u>ay</u>s	w<u>ei</u>ght	tr<u>ai</u>n
h<u>ea</u>d	s<u>ai</u>d	v<u>e</u>ry	j<u>ea</u>lous
gr<u>ea</u>t	h<u>ea</u>lth	<u>a</u>nywhere	expl<u>ai</u>ns

/e/	/eɪ/
let	cake

T12.5 Listen and check your answers.

▶▶ p63

Word focus

Words with silent letters

1 These words all contain silent letters. Cross out the silent letters like this:

ghost   i̸sland   k̸now   w̸ho

castle	comb	wrist
daughter	might	fruit
opera	cupboard	bought
listen	foreigner	friend
designer	handsome	suit
whale	lamb	white
could	night	wrong
scissors	cheque	two
answer	champagne	yoghurt

T12.6 Listen and check your answers.

▶▶ p63

2 Listen again and repeat the words. Make sure you don't pronounce the silent letters.

3 Work on your own. Write sentences using as many of the words in 1 as you can.

Examples
There might be more than two ghosts in the castle.
Who bought the fruit yoghurt in the cupboard?
The handsome foreigner wore a white suit.
The opera designer drank champagne all night.

4 Work with a partner. Exchange sentences. Practise reading your partner's sentences aloud as fast as you can.

Connected speech

Linking in phrasal verbs

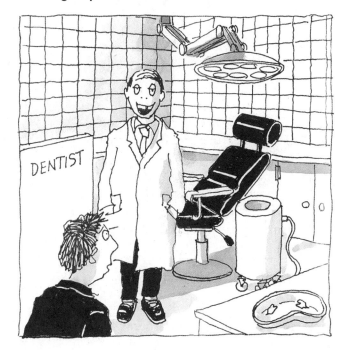

1 **T12.7** Listen and complete the sentences with phrasal verbs.

1 Please ___come in___ , I was ___waiting for___ you.

2 I'm afraid I _____ yesterday.

3 I'll _____ the bottles when
I _____ the children.

4 I _____ but it isn't in the dictionary.

5 Where are your gloves? _____ before
you _____ .

> **T12.8** Phrasal verbs are often difficult to understand because of linking. Listen.
>
> Throw‿it‿away!

▶▶ p63
▶▶ p63

2 Mark the linking in these sentences.

1 (Put them on!)

2 (Take them off!)

3 (Pick them up!)

4 (Turn it off!)

5 (Switch it on!)

6 (Fill it in!)

7 (Work it out!)

8 (Put it down!)

9 (Look it up!)

T12.9 Listen and check your answers.

▶▶ p63

3 Now practise the sentences. Pay attention to linking.

4 **T12.10** Listen to people telling you what to do. Respond to each sentence the same way as **B**.

Example

A

(Put on your coat.)
You hear

(I've already put it on.)
You say

B

(I've already put it on.)
You hear

▶▶ p63

13

The sound /h/
Syllable counting
Four-syllable words
Corrective stress

Sounds

The sound /h/

1 Circle the words in the box below which contain the sound /h/.

somewhere	what	hospital	hours
hotel	happy	why	when
who	honest	heaven	which
half	homeless	exhausted	hurts

T13.1 Listen and check your answers. You will only hear the words with the sound /h/.

▶▶ p63

> To make the sound /h/, open your mouth and push air out. /h/ is a soft sound. (Don't make it hard or use your voice.)

2 Listen to the /h/ words from 1. Practise saying them.

3 **T13.2** Listen to some students saying these sentences. Circle the /h/ sounds which they don't pronounce correctly.

1 His house is at the top of the hill.

2 Hello, Peter! How are you?

3 It's very hot in here.

4 He's in hospital.

5 I've got a horrible headache.

6 I had a hamburger for lunch.

7 My hotel's near the school.

8 My husband's a doctor.

9 How did you get home?

▶▶ p63

4 Work with a partner. Put these sentences into the correct order. There may be more than one possibility.

1 helped / I / have / ?

    Have I helped?

2 hamburgers / hate / eating / I / !

   _____

3 in / Abigail / here / hoovered / has / ?

   _____

4 Aunt Hannah / Alan Harbord / his / adores / .

   _____

5 heart attack / had / Harriet Elston / old / a / .

   _____

6 Helmut / Anna / hurriedly / about / asked / English / homework / his / .

   _____

T13.3 Listen and compare your answers with the sentences on the recording.

▶▶ p63

5 Listen again and repeat the sentences. Pay attention to the correct pronunciation of the /h/ sounds.

> Take care *not* to pronounce /h/ sounds in front of words that begin with vowel sounds. Link the last sound of the word before with these vowels instead.
>
> Example
> *not* → Have /h/ I helped?
> but → Have ‿I helped?

Word focus

Counting syllables

1 **T13.4** Listen and count the number of syllables in these words.

businessmen	3	favourite	☐
chocolate	☐	interested	☐
comfortable	☐	marriage	☐
conference	☐	medicine	☐
delicious	☐	millionaire	☐
dictionary	☐	miserable	☐
different	☐	restaurant	☐
documentary	☐	several	☐
fashionable	☐	temperature	☐

2 Listen again and practise the words. Do not add any extra syllables.

3 **T13.5** Listen to some students saying the sentences below.

Tick (✓) the sentence if the underlined words are pronounced correctly.

Cross (✗) the sentence if the underlined words are pronounced incorrectly.

1 This chocolate is delicious!

2 Are you interested in marriage?

3 Here's some medicine for your temperature.

4 It's a fashionable restaurant.

5 He's a miserable millionaire.

6 It's a different sort of dictionary.

7 Several businessmen were there.

8 It was a documentary about a sales conference.

9 She felt comfortable in her favourite chair.

4 **T13.6** Listen and repeat the sentences with the correct pronunciation.

Four-syllable words

1 Do you know what these words mean? Check any words that you don't know in a dictionary.

absolutely	decorator	fortunately
advertising	disappointing	graduated
biography	education	impossible
communicate	efficiently	independence
concentrating	everybody	optimistic
conversation	extravagant	supermarket

2 Put the words into this table, according to their stress pattern.

• ● • •	● • • •	• • ● •
		absolutely

T13.7 Listen and check your answers.

▶▶ p64

3 Listen again and repeat the words, paying attention to stress.

4 Make a list of as many four-syllable words as you can. How many of these words can you add to each box?

When you finish, use a dictionary to check the stress pattern of words you are not sure of.

Intonation and sentence stress

Corrective stress

T13.8 Listen. We often stress words strongly when we correct people.

1 **T13.9** Look at these dialogues. Listen and mark the main stress ■ in each **B** reply.

1 **A** So, the address is Mr P Blake, 46 Shakespeare Close, London SW3?

  B No, it's Mr P Blake, 46 Shakespeare Road, London SW3.

2 **A** So, the address is Mr P Blake, 46 Milton Road, London SW3?

  B No, it's Mr P Blake, 46 Shakespeare Road, London SW3.

3 **A** So, the address is Mrs P Blake, 46 Shakespeare Road, London SW3?

  B No, it's Mr P Blake, 46 Shakespeare Road, London SW3.

4 **A** So, the address is Mr P Drake, 46 Shakespeare Road, London SW3?

  B No, it's Mr P Blake, 46 Shakespeare Road, London SW3.

5 **A** So, the address is Mr P Blake, 46 Shakespeare Road, London SW4?

  B No, it's Mr P Blake, 46 Shakespeare Road, London SW3.

6 **A** So, the address is Mr P Blake, 47 Shakespeare Road, London SW3?

  B No, it's Mr P Blake, 46 Shakespeare Road, London SW3.

▶▶ p64

2 Listen again and repeat the answers. Read the dialogues aloud with a partner. Pay attention to the stress.

3 Brian gets a lot of wrong number phone calls. Look at Brian's answers below. The stress is in a different place each time. Can you write a question for each answer?

1

Hello. Is that 659 2590 ___ ?

No, it's 659 0590.

2

___ ?

No, it's 659 0590.

3

___ ?

No, it's 659 0590.

4

___ ?

No, it's 659 0590.

5

___ ?

No, it's 659 0590.

6

___ ?

No, it's 659 0590.

►► p64

4 Read your dialogues aloud with a partner.

14

The sounds /ɒ/, /ɔ:/, and /əʊ/
Words often confused because of their pronunciation
Hearing 'd (had or would)

Sounds

The sounds /ɒ/, /ɔ:/, and /əʊ/

T14.1 The sounds /ɒ/, /ɔ:/, and /əʊ/ are easy to confuse. Listen and make sure you can hear the difference.

fox   cock

forks   cork

folks   Coke

1 **T14.2** You will hear ten words. Listen, and for each word, put a tick (✓) in the correct box according to the sound you hear.

	/ɒ/	/ɔ:/	/əʊ/	
1	✓	☐	☐	clock
2	☐	☐	☐	
3	☐	☐	☐	
4	☐	☐	☐	
5	☐	☐	☐	
6	☐	☐	☐	
7	☐	☐	☐	
8	☐	☐	☐	
9	☐	☐	☐	
10	☐	☐	☐	

2 Listen again and write the words you hear in the gaps.

►► p64

3 Look at the words in this box. Use a dictionary to check the meaning of any words that you are not sure of.

wa<u>l</u>k	wr<u>o</u>ng	w<u>o</u>n't	g<u>o</u>ne
ag<u>o</u>	n<u>o</u>vel	w<u>a</u>ter	<u>a</u>ll
qu<u>a</u>rrel	w<u>a</u>nt	<u>o</u>nly	d<u>oo</u>r
m<u>o</u>ment	th<u>ou</u>ght	ph<u>o</u>ne	alth<u>ou</u>gh

4 Put the words in the columns below according to the sound of the underlined letters.

/ɒ/	/ɔ:/	/əʊ/
	walk	

T14.3 Listen and check your answers.

►► p64

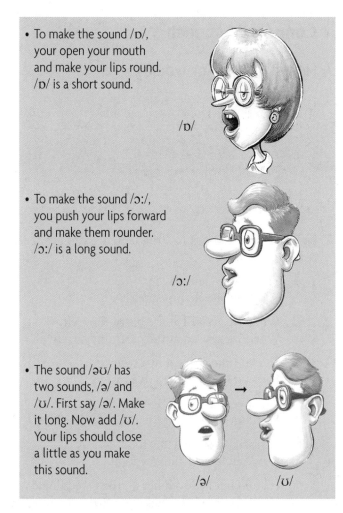

- To make the sound /ɒ/, your open your mouth and make your lips round. /ɒ/ is a short sound.

/ɒ/

- To make the sound /ɔː/, you push your lips forward and make them rounder. /ɔː/ is a long sound.

/ɔː/

- The sound /əʊ/ has two sounds, /ə/ and /ʊ/. First say /ə/. Make it long. Now add /ʊ/. Your lips should close a little as you make this sound.

/ə/   /ʊ/

5 Read the words in 3 with the recording.

6 With a partner you are going to play the game 'Space Battle'. In this game you try to find and hit your partner's spaceships.

These are the spaceships:

| X | flying saucer (= 5 points) |

| X | X | X | rocket (= 20 points) |

space station (= 50 points)

Don't let your partner see your grid. On the grid marked *You*, put crosses where your spaceships are. You can put your rockets and your space station horizontally (→) or vertically (↓).

You each have:
4 flying saucers   2 rockets   1 space station

When you have put all your spaceships in your grid, you are ready to play the game. (Don't put anything in the grid marked *Your partner* yet.)

Student A Student B will say the name of a square on your grid. Shade the square like this . If there is a ✗ in the square, say HIT. If there is no ✗, say MISS. If the HIT is a flying saucer or the last remaining square of a bigger spaceship, say HIT AND DESTROYED. (The shaded squares show you the squares your partner has already called.)

Example

sport, coat   HIT!

Student B On the grid marked *Your partner*, try to find Student A's spaceships. Say the name of a square on the grid where you think there is a spaceship. If Student A says HIT, draw a ✗. If they say MISS, draw a ◯ .

Now take it in turns to ask and answer. After ten minutes stop the game and see who has the most points. (You only get points for the spaceships you have destroyed.)

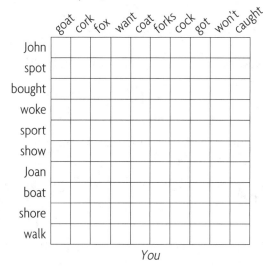

You

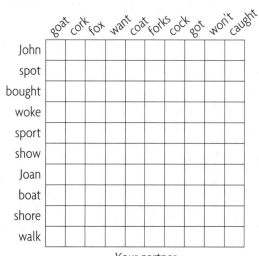

Your partner

Word focus

Words often confused because of their pronunciation

1 These pairs of words are often confused. Check the meaning of any words you don't know in a dictionary.

1	chef	chief	5	dessert desert
2	chicken	kitchen	6	quite quiet
3	walk	work	7	recipe receipt
4	soup	soap	8	dairy diary

T14.4 Listen and repeat the pairs of words.

2 Circle the correct word in each sentence.

1 Sitting Bull was a very famous North American Indian *chef* / *chief*.

2 They've got a very modern *chicken* / *kitchen* in their flat.

3 I *walk* / *work* as a computer programmer at IBM.

4 This beef and onion *soup* / *soap* is delicious!

5 They rode their camels across the *dessert* / *desert*.

6 Our bedroom's very *quite* / *quiet*. You can't hear the noise of the motorway at all from there.

7 Is there a *recipe* / *receipt* for chocolate cake in that book?

8 Just let me check in my *diary* / *dairy* to see if I'm free next Wednesday.

T14.5 Listen and check your answers.

►► p64

3 Listen again, and say the sentences with the circled words.

Connected speech

Hearing *'d* (*had* or *would*)

> *'d* is the contracted form of *had* and *would*.
>
> **Example**
> I'd like an ice-cream. = *would*
> I felt I'd been there before. = *had*
>
> Sometimes it can be difficult to hear *'d* in a sentence.

1 **T14.6** Listen and tick (✓) the sentence you hear each time.

1 a I really like champagne.
  b I'd really like champagne. ✓

2 a When we arrived at the party, they left.
  b When we arrived at the party, they'd left.

3 a She said she worked in a casino.
  b She said she'd worked in a casino.

4 a You love Marsha!
  b You'd love Marsha!

5 a He asked if we had any food.
  b He asked if we'd had any food.

6 a He told her he loved her on their wedding day.
  b He told her he'd loved her on their wedding day.

7 a I said they lived in Spain!
  b I said they'd lived in Spain!

►► p64

2 **T14.7** Listen and repeat these pairs of verbs. Try to make the *'d* as clear as possible.

I like	…	I'd like
you love	…	you'd love
she worked	…	she'd worked
he loved	…	he'd loved
we had	…	we'd had
they left	…	they'd left
they lived	…	they'd lived

3 Work with a partner.

Student A Read seven of the sentences in 1 aloud.
Student B Point to the sentence you hear each time.

When you have finished, swap roles.

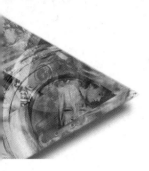

Sound symbol chart

/p/	/t/	/k/	/f/	/s/	/θ/	/ʃ/	/tʃ/
/b/	/d/	/g/	/v/	/z/	/ð/	/ʒ/	/dʒ/
/h/	/l/	/r/	/w/	/m/	/n/	/ŋ/	/j/
/ɪ/	/i:/	/u:/	/ʊ/	/eɪ/	/ɪə/	/əʊ/	
/ə/	/ɜ:/	/ɔ:/	/ɒ/	/aɪ/	/eə/	/aʊ/	
/e/	/æ/	/ɑ:/	/ʌ/	/ɔɪ/	/ʊə/		

Note Words like *happy* and *hungry* end in a short sound halfway between /i:/ and /ɪ/. Some dictionaries show this as /i/.

Tom   Joe   Paul   Liz   Sue   Jane

1 Transcribe the following sentences.

1 /tɒm laɪks 'raɪtɪŋ 'pəʊətri/

   Tom likes writing poetry.

2 /dʒeɪnz gɒt ə 'frendli braʊn pet kæt/

_____

3 /su: wəz fɑ:st ə'sli:p wen ðə 'bɜ:gləz keɪm/

_____

4 /dʒəʊ bɔ:t ə 'bɒtəl əv hʌŋ'geəriən waɪn lɑ:st naɪt/

_____

5 /lɪz wɒnts tə bi: rɪtʃ ənd 'feɪməs wʌn deɪ/

_____

6 /pɔ:lz ə 'welθi jʌŋ 'tʊərɪst/

_____

7 /tɒm ənd lɪz ə gʊd ət 'spænɪʃ/

_____

8 /dʒəʊ wɜ:ks ɪn ə 'nɔɪzi 'gærɑ:ʒ/

_____

T15 Listen and check your answers.

▶▶ p64

Key

Unit 1

Consonant symbols 1

1 `T1.3`

/p/	play	/s/	study
/b/	book	/z/	music
/t/	teacher	/h/	hot
/d/	drive	/l/	letter
/k/	can	/r/	room
/g/	go	/m/	mean
/f/	flat	/n/	never
/v/	van	/w/	work

2 The symbols in Picture A are for sounds made without the voice. (See Diagram 2.) They are called 'voiceless' sounds. The symbols in Picture B are for sounds made with the voice. (See Diagram 1.) They are called 'voiced' sounds.

3
1	✗ /w/	5	✓	9	✓
2	✓	6	✗ /f/	10	✗ /z/
3	✓	7	✓	11	✓
4	✗ /s/	8	✓	12	✗ /r/

Word linking

1 `T1.6`

1 I don't really speak Italian. (6 words)
2 I'm going to work as a translator. (8 words)
3 We've got three children. (5 words)
4 My husband's English. (4 words)
5 I'm enjoying my course a lot. (7 words)

5 `T1.10`

1 a message‿in‿a bottle
2 anger‿and‿other‿emotions
3 a lot‿of‿information

4 How‿is‿it possible?
5 quickly‿and‿easily
6 words‿on‿a page

Intonation in *Wh-* and *Yes/No* questions

1 `T1.11`

1 Where do you live, Eva?*
2 When's your birthday, Pablo?*
3 Do you have a job, Kimiko?
4 What sort of music do you like, Stefan?*
5 Have you got any brothers or sisters, Maria?
6 Can you speak three languages, Xavier?
7 How do you come to school, Fatima?*
8 Do you like dancing, Maurizio?
* = *Wh-* questions

2 Statement 1 is **false**.
Statement 2 is **true**.

Unit 2

The sounds /s/, /z/, and /ɪz/

3 `T2.1`

Group 1 /s/: gets, makes, puts, bakes, invites, surfs, likes, hopes
Group 2 /z/: tries, calls, goes, does, orders, spends, drives, lives, reads, plays, loves
Group 3 /ɪz/: washes, teaches, manages, misses, loses

5 1 You pronounce the ending /ɪz/ if the verb ends in one of the following sounds: /s/, /z/, /ʃ/, /tʃ/, /dʒ/.

2 If the verb ends in any other voiceless consonant sound, you pronounce the ending /s/.
3 If the verb ends in any other voiced consonant sound or a vowel sound, you pronounce the ending /z/.

Two-syllable nouns

2
1	champagne	7	coffee
2	sardines	8	apples
3	cartoons	9	paintings
4	Japan	10	Britain
5	guitars	11	trumpets
6	shampoo	12	toothpaste

3 She likes the objects on the left because they are all stressed on the second syllable, like her name:

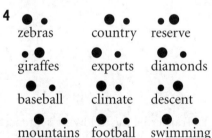

The usual stress pattern for two-syllable nouns is ● •.

Strong and weak forms of auxiliary verbs

2 1 Yes, she does.
2 Yes, she has.
3 Yes, she was.
4 Yes, she can.
5 Yes, they were.
6 Yes, they do.
7 Yes, they have.

3 The auxiliary verbs are in the table in this order: *do, does, have, has, were, was,* and *can.*

4 1 Does Janet live in Spain?
Yes, she does.

2 Has she got a job?
Yes, she has.

3 Was she born in England?
Yes, she was.

4 Can she speak Spanish?
Yes, she can.

5 Were they married in Spain?
Yes, they were.

6 Do they share the housework?
Yes, they do.

7 Have they got any children?
Yes, they have.

5 1 W W   4 W W   7 W W
2 W S   5 W S
3 W S   6 W S

Unit 3

Pronunciation of *-ed* past tenses

2 Bert: 1, 5, 7, 9
Fred: 2, 4, 8, 10, 12
David: 3, 6, 11

4 `T3.3`
/t/: walked, laughed, watched, washed
/d/: answered, planned, showed, tried, believed, carried
/ɪd/: mended, started

5 `T3.5`
         /t/
1 She walked‿all day.
         /t/
2 We watched‿it carefully.
              /d/
3 They answered‿everybody's questions.
       /d/
4 He tried‿a piece.
              /d/
5 They planned‿it weeks ago.
          /t/
6 It washed‿all the glasses beautifully.

Saying years

1 1 1492   4 1990   7 1960
2 1616   5 1939
3 1918   6 1815

2
1 1314 = thirteen fourteen
2 1410 = fourteen ten
3 1492 = fourteen ninety-two
4 1504 = fifteen oh four
5 1616 = sixteen sixteen
6 1713 = seventeen thirteen
7 1780 = seventeen eighty
8 1815 = eighteen fifteen
9 1840 = eighteen forty
10 1900 = nineteen hundred
11 1918 = nineteen eighteen
12 1939 = nineteen thirty-nine
13 1960 = nineteen sixty
14 1990 = nineteen ninety

The *-teen* words are stressed ●● when they come at the beginning of dates, and ●● when they come at the end of dates. (The key for the exercise shows the main stress in each *-teen* word, or other part of the date.)

Strong and weak forms of prepositions

1 1 to   6 of   11 of
2 from   7 at   12 from
3 for   8 to   13 for
4 at   9 for
5 to   10 for

Because they come in the middle of sentences and are not stressed, these prepositions are all weak in pronunciation.

2

	Weak forms	Strong forms
to	/tə/	/tuː/
from	/frəm/	/frɒm/
for	/fə/ or /fər/	/fɔː/
at	/ət/	/æt/
of	/əv/	/ɒv/

Unit 4

Single vowel symbols

1 The vowels in Picture A are long. The vowels in Picture B are short.

2, 3 `T4.2`
1 /iː/ teacher   7 /ɑː/ car
2 /ɪ/ kitchen   8 /ʌ/ study
3 /ɜː/ work   9 /ɔː/ ball
4 /ə/ cinema   10 /ɒ/ hot
5 /uː/ who   11 /e/ pen
6 /ʊ/ book   12 /æ/ cat

4 The following are the words that *do not* contain the vowel sound on the left. The correct vowel sound is given on the right.

1 /e/   woman ✗ (ə ✓)
2 /ʌ/   sugar ✗ (ʊ ✓)
3 /ɒ/   onion ✗ (ʌ ✓)
4 /ɜː/ pork ✗ (ɔː ✓)
5 /iː/ wine ✗ (aɪ ✓)
6 /ɑː/ carrots ✗ (æ ✓)
7 /ɪ/   birds ✗ (ɜː ✓)
8 /uː/ look ✗ (ʊ ✓)

5 1 bus /ʌ/   6 shop /ɒ/
2 tall /ɔː/   7 apples /æ/
3 word /ɜː/   8 blue /uː/
4 good /ʊ/   9 cigarette /ə/
5 park /ɑː/

6 1 black   6 school
2 butter   7 girl
3 pot   8 stores
4 club   9 car
5 eggs   10 key

Containers

1 1 a bottle of wine/lemonade
2 a packet of sugar/crisps
3 a box of matches/chocolates
4 a tin of sardines/tomatoes
5 a can of cola/beer
6 a jar of coffee/jam

7 a tube of toothpaste/glue
8 a carton of eggs/juice

Note Perhaps it's different in your country, but you can often buy these things in these containers in Britain.

2 `T4.5`

A So, what do we need for the party?
B Erm … six cans of beer … a couple of cartons of orange juice …
A Right.
B Two bottles of wine – one red, one white.
A OK.
B Maybe two packets of crisps.
A What flavour?
B Cheese and onion.
A Fine.
B And a tin of black olives.
A Right. And do we need anything for the house?
B Let me think: Yes, A big jar of coffee, and erm … a box of kitchen matches. Oh, yes, and a small tube of glue.

6 cans of <u>beer</u>
a couple of cartons of <u>orange juice</u>
2 bottles of wine (1 red, 1 <u>white</u>)
2 packets of crisps (<u>cheese and onion</u> flavour)
a tin of <u>black</u> olives
a <u>big</u> jar of coffee
a box of <u>kitchen</u> matches
a <u>small</u> tube of glue

List intonation

1 `T4.7`

1	trousers	9	underpants
2	skirt	10	shoes
3	swimming trunks	11	boots
4	T-shirt	12	blouse
5	knickers	13	pyjamas
6	shirt	14	bra
7	dress	15	tie
8	dressing gown		

2 Pattern **1** is the intonation pattern for lists. The intonation always goes down on the last item (to show the list is finished), and up on all the items that come before the last (to show there are more items to come).

3 `T4.9`

A My sister Sally went to the summer sales and she bought a pink tie.
B … a pink tie and a grey blouse.
C … a pink tie, a grey blouse, and a white skirt.
D … a pink tie, a grey blouse, a white skirt, and some brown shoes.

Unit 5

The sound /w/

1 `T5.1`

warm	worried
world	watch
languages	questions
when	

Note
The words lea<u>v</u>ing, <u>v</u>iews, hea<u>v</u>y, <u>v</u>iolence, and fa<u>v</u>ourite contain /v/ sounds.

In the word t<u>w</u>o the letter *w* is silent.

In the following words, the letter *w* represents a rounded vowel or diphthong:

/əʊ/ own, borrow
/aʊ/ how
/uː/ views

2 The sentences in which /w/ is pronounced **incorrectly** are:

1 wine /vaɪn/ ✗
2 would /gwʊd/ ✗
5 wheel /fiːl/ ✗

5 1 b   2 d   3 a   4 c

Rhythm and /ə/

1 `T5.5`

• • •
Pippa's going to travel round the world.

• • •
Hannah's going to stay at home.

• • • •
Peter's going to join a punk rock band.

• • •
And Richard's going to teach in Rome.

• • •
Amanda's going to move to Hollywood

• • •
Where she hopes to become a star.

• • •
Frank's going to pass his driving test,

• • •
And then he's going to buy himself a car.

• • •
Paula's going to study up at Cambridge,

• • •
And Roger's going to learn how to cook.

Emma's going to have a lot of babies,

And Sarah's going to write a book.

Steven's going to be a scientist

And try to help the human race.

Helen's going to be in the Olympic team

And finish in the long jump in first place.

2 *line 3* = 10 syllables   *line 11* = 8 syllables
  line 6 = 7 syllables   *line 12* = 10 syllables
  line 7 = 9 syllables   *line 14* = 9 syllables
  line 8 = 8 syllables   *line 19* = 11 syllables

4
                /ə/   /ə/   /ə/   /ə/
  line 7   Peter's going to join a punk rock band
                /ə/   /ə/   /ə/   /ə/
  line 8   And Richard's going to teach in Rome
                      /ə/   /ə/
  line 11   Frank's going to pass his driving test
              /ə/   /ə/   /ə/   /ə/
  line 12   And then he's going to buy himself a car
              /ə/   /ə/   /ə/   /ə/   /ə/
  line 14   And Roger's going to learn how to cook
              /ə/   /ə/   /ə/   /ə/
  line 19   Helen's going to be in the Olympic team

5 **Note**
The number of stresses is more important than the number of syllables in making an English sentence long or short to say. Because of this, you can say lines 3, 7, 11, and 19 (which have four stresses) in the same amount of time, or lines 6, 8, 12, and 14 (which have three stresses), in the same amount of time. The four-stressed lines will all take a little longer to say than the three-stressed lines.

Hearing the difference between polite and impolite offers

2   1   **Paul**   I'll iron it for you.
     2   **Assistant**   I'll get it for you in a moment.
     3   **Secretary**   I'll buy some now.
     4   **Nick**   I'll do it for you.
     5   **Mechanic**   I'll have a look at the engine for you.

3   1 P   2 P   3 I   4 P   5 I

5   1   I'll get some for you.   3   I'll clean them for you.
     2   I'll carry it for you.   4   I'll buy it for you.

Unit 6

The sounds /n/ and /ŋ/ (and /ŋg/ and /ndʒ/)

2   **T6.2**
/n/: winter, friendly, modern, pond, children, newsagent, window, expensive
/ŋ/: sink, junk, think, thanks, drink, ankle, bank, uncle

3   The letter *n* is pronounced /ŋ/ when the following sound is /k/.

5   **T6.4**

/ŋ/	/ŋg/	/ndʒ/
thing	hungry	danger
singing	stronger	strange
wedding	English	oranges
young	single	changing
darling	bungalow	exchanged
wrong	congratulations	
buildings		
king		

6   The letters *ng* at the end of a word are always pronounced /ŋ/.

Note
We say the adjectives *long*, *strong*, and *young* with a final /ŋ/. We say the comparative and superlative forms with /ŋgə/ or /ŋgɪst/.

Apart from these exceptions, words with a final /ŋ/ do not change pronunciation when endings are added.

Example
ring   /rɪŋ/   →   *ringing*   /ˈrɪŋɪŋ/
sing   /sɪŋ/   →   *singer*   /ˈsɪŋə/
young   /jʌŋ/   →   *youngish*   /ˈjʌŋɪʃ/

7   **T6.5**
     1   He's stro /ŋ/ er than Hercules.
     2   Can't you see anythin /ŋk/?
     3   Are you enjoying it here? ✓
     4   I'll ri /ŋg/ up later.
     5   He goes joggin / / every day.
     6   My brother often goes fishing. ✓

8   The matched-up dialogues are as follows:
     1 and c (practising /n/, /ŋ/, and /ŋk/)
     2 and d (practising /n/ and /ŋg/)
     3 and a (practising /ndʒ/, /m/, and /n/)
     4 and b (practising /ŋ/, /n/, /ŋg/, and /m/)

Three-syllable words

3, 4

●●● Melanie	●●● Rebecca	●●● Bernadette
looks	beautiful	good-looking	overweight
character	sociable	romantic	impolite
job	journalist	musician	unemployed
favourite food	sausages	tomatoes	carrot soup
favourite city	Birmingham	Bologna	Aberdeen

The best girlfriend for Luigi is Rebecca. She's good-looking and he's attractive. She's romantic and he's old-fashioned. She's a musician and he's artistic. She likes Bologna and he's Italian.

5

1 She's a magazine journalist.

2 We waited in the airport for seventeen hours.

3 Who wants to be a millionaire?

4 We've got a second-hand car.

5 Todd's only seventeen.

6 Mr Green was a millionaire businessman.

7 *Arena*'s my favourite magazine.

8 I bought my computer second hand.

Hearing different forms of *like*

1 1 b   2 a   3 b   4 a   5 b   6 a

2 T6.12
1 She's very like her mother.
2 He doesn't like his elder sister.
3 I'd like to live in London.
4 What would you like to drink?
5 He isn't like anyone in his family.
6 Does she like you?

Unit 7

Consonant symbols 2

2 /ʃ/ sugar, special   /θ/ south, birthday
/ʒ/ usually, pleasure   /ð/ together, this
/tʃ/ matches, cheap   /j/ you, Europe
/dʒ/ changed, just   /ŋ/ drunk, long

5 1 a   2 c   3 b   4 c   5 a   6 c   7 a   8 b

The sounds /θ/ and /ð/

1 T7.5
/θ/: north, health, things, months, three, athlete
/ð/: grandfather, other, them, clothes, their, leather

3 T7.6
A Sorry I broke /d/ ose plates.
B That's all right. I didn't really like them. ✓
C /z/ ere are your /s/ eatre tickets!
D /t/ anks a lot.
E It's Tom's birthday on Thursday. ✓
F Yes, and I haven't got him anything. ✓
G Do you like my lea /z/ er trousers?
H I think they're great! ✓
I How much is that watch wor /s/?
J About /f/ irty pounds.
K This music's boring. ✓
L Shh! My bro /d/ er likes /v/ e Beatles.

Present Perfect and Past Simple – the pronunciation of *'s*

1 1 b   2 a   3 b   4 b   5 a   6 a   7 a

2 In sentences 1, 2, 4, and 7 *'s* is prounced /z/. This is because it follows a vowel sound or a voiced consonant sound.

In sentences 3, 5, 6, and 8 *'s* is pronounced /s/. This is because it follows one of the voiceless consonants /f/, /k/, /t/, or /p/.

Note
When *has* follows the sounds /s/, /z/, /tʃ/, /dʒ/, /ʃ/, or /ʒ/, we do not write it as a contraction, and we pronounce it as /həz/ or /əz/.

Example
/tʃ/ The match has finished.
/dʒ/ The bridge has fallen down.

3 Pronounce the *'s* as /s/ in Present Perfect sentences 1, 5, and 6.
Pronounce the *'s* as /z/ in Present Perfect sentences 3 and 4.

Unit 8

The sounds /ʃ/, /s/, and /tʃ/

2 1 chef   4 profession
2 special   5 receptionist
3 sure   6 ocean

3 T8.3
1 ship   chip   ship
2 she   sea   sea

3 choose shoes shoes
4 short sort short
5 catch catch cash
6 sew show sew
7 washing watching watching
8 seat sheet sheet

7 The underlined letters are pronounced /ʃ/.

1 Engli**sh** **sh**oppers **sh**ort of ca**sh** (4)
2 Swedi**sh** fa**sh**ion **sh**ow **sh**ocks Briti**sh** (5)
3 Infla**ti**on hits Ru**ss**ian **ch**ampagne (3)
4 Ambi**ti**ous Sco**tti**sh recep**ti**onist **sh**oots boss (4)
5 Iri**sh** fi**sh**ing **sh**ip sinks in Pacific O**ce**an (4)

The sounds /ʊ/ and /uː/

2 1 same   5 different
2 different   6 different
3 same   7 different
4 different   8 same

4 1 'fool'   3 Luke
2 'Pull'   4 soot

6 a r**oo**m with a v**iew**
an afforn**oo**n cr**uise**
W**ou**ld y**ou** like n**ew** b**oo**ts?
a f**ew** q**ueue**s
fr**ui**t with s**u**gar
a sh**oe** m**u**seum
a l**oo**k at the w**oo**ds
fond**ue**s or barbec**ue**s
b**oo**k through Thomas C**oo**k
g**oo**d f**oo**d
I sh**ou**ldn't be r**u**de
Y**ou** c**ou**ldn't d**o** better

Questions with *or*

1 Intonation pattern 4 is the correct pattern for *or* questions.

2 Dialogue 2 is the most formal.
Dialogue 3 is the most unfriendly.
Dialogue 1 is informal but friendly.

3 **T8.9**
1 **A** Do you want tea or coffee?
  B Oh, coffee, please.

A Black or white?
B White, please.
A With sugar or without?
B Oh, no sugar for me, please.

2 **C** Would you like beer or wine with the meal?
  D Mmm … I think wine would be nice.
  C All right. Would you prefer red or white?
  D Erm … white, I think.

3 **E** Next, please. Can I help you?
  F A hamburger and a Coke, please.
  E Large or regular Coke?
  F Regular, please.
  E To eat here or take away?
  F Take away, please.

Unit 9

The sounds /iː/ and /ɪ/

2 **T9.1**
1 feet   6 bins
2 seat   7 Tim
3 still   8 cheap
4 feel   9 pitch
5 gins   10 live

4 1 gins   4 bins
2 feel   5 leave
3 Tim   6 peach

5 **T9.3**
/iː/ (the boxed words): week, me, visa, people, season

/ɪ/ (the circled words): business, finished, enough, message, remember, bicycles, trip

Word counting and sentence stress patterns

1 1 8   4 8   7 7
2 9   5 9   8 9
3 7   6 6

2 **T9.4**
1 If she asks, I'll tell her everything.
2 What'll you do if they don't arrive?

3 I'll write if I have time.
4 We'll phone if the bus is late.
5 How will they get here if it's snowing?
6 If she goes, will you stay?
7 We'll take you if you like.
8 I won't come if you don't want.

4 4 d   5 b   6 e   7 a   8 c

Showing interest and surprise

2 1 Is she?   7 Has she?
2 Does she?   8 Is there?
3 Did it?   9 Are you?
4 Can she?   10 Have you?
5 Has she?   11 Do they?
6 Is it?   12 Do you?

Unit 10

Diphthong symbols

1 1 bear, hair   5 deer, beer
2 fly, tie   6 crow, hello
3 cow, bow   7 Grey, way
4 boy, toy   8 Moor, tour

4 /eɪ/ train, way
/aɪ/ buy, try
/ɔɪ/ enjoyed, noisy
/ɪə/ here, clear
/eə/ repair, there
/əʊ/ only, home
/aʊ/ brown, house
/ʊə/ poor, sure

5 1 b   3 a   5 b   7 b
2 a   4 c   6 c   8 c

Strong form prepositions at the end of questions

1 1 at   4 from   7 to
2 at   5 in   8 to
3 about   6 off

2 **T10.6**
1 Who did he smile at?
2 What did they talk about?
3 Where did he come from?
4 What was he interested in?
5 Where did he get off?

6 Who did the book belong to?

7 Which address did she write to?

Contractions

1 **T10.7**

1 You shouldn't eat fatty foods.

2 She can't speak Italian very well.

3 **A** You haven't read it, have you?

  B Yes, I have.[1]

4 There's a bus stop opposite the library.

5 Sean would like to be an astronaut.[2]

6 I'm right, aren't I?

7 It'll be the biggest city on earth.

8 What are your names?[3]

9 Who is it?[4]

10 I didn't use to watch much TV as a child.

Further notes on the writing and pronunciation of contractions

[1] We do not write or pronounce contractions in short affirmative answers. Short negative answers are written and pronounced with contractions (eg *No, I haven't.*).

[2] We can write many different contractions with personal pronouns (eg *she'd, he's, we're, it'll, they've,* etc.). With nouns the only usual written contraction is *'s* (for *has* or *is*). In sentences like *Sean would like to be an astronaut. The plane will land in half an hour,* or *The children have arrived,* we pronounce the contractions, but we do not write them.

[3] With non-personal pronouns the only usual written contraction is *'s* (for *has* or *is*). (Other possible written contractions with non-personal pronouns are *what'll, that'll, who'll,* and *who'd.*) In questions like *What are your names?* or *Where have you been?,* we pronounce the contractions, but we do not write them.

[4] We do not write or pronounce *'s* contractions with short *Wh*-questions ending in the word *it*. With words like *that* or *this* at the end, contractions are possible (eg *What's that?, Where's that?, Who's this?*).

Unit 11

The sounds /e/, /æ/, and /ʌ/

2 **T11.1**

1	beg	5	Ben	9	ton
2	bag	6	sex	10	bed
3	bug	7	sucks	11	bed
4	ban	8	tan		

9 1 = bookshop   10 = cinema
8 = butcher's   2 = hospital
6 = church   12 = hotel

T11.5

A Where's the bookshop?

B In Benbury Street, on the corner of Beddington Road.

A Where's the butcher's?

B In Saxton Arcade.

A Where's the church?

B In Banbury Street, on the corner of Baddington Road.

A Where's the cinema?

B In Bunbury Street, on the corner of Tonbridge Gardens.

A Where's the hospital?

B In Bug Lane.

A Where's the hotel?

B In Bunbury Street, on the corner of Tanbridge Gardens.

Word linking

1 **T11.8**

Most people's picture_of_a typical_Englishman_is_a man _in_a suit, with_an_umbrella, a copy_of *The Times,* and_a *bowler* hat. Not_everyone knows, however, that this hard, low, round-brimmed hat was _invented_in the nineteenth century, or that_it was named _after_a pair_of British hat makers, Thomas_and William Bowler.

The first_example_of_a bowler hat was_ordered by_a country gentleman, Thomas Coke, who lived_in Norfolk. He wanted_a strong_and practical hat that he could wear when he went_out shooting.

In_America the bowler hat_is known_as_a *derby.*

Weak form auxiliaries and passive verbs

3 The missing words are underlined.

T11.10

A cleaning woman, Mrs Ethel Boggis, <u>was</u> shot in a bank robbery in Cricklewood yesterday evening. She <u>is</u> said to be safe and comfortable in hospital. The bank <u>was</u> broken into by two masked men. They have not yet <u>been</u> found. A total of £1 million <u>was</u> stolen in the robbery, and a bag of jewels <u>was</u> also taken. The jewels <u>were</u> kept in a bank safe by Lady Agatha Crickle who <u>was</u> told the bad news late last night by the bank manager.

'Most of my jewels <u>were</u> made of gold,' she told reporters. 'My favourite ring <u>was</u> made in China three hundred years ago. I can't possibly buy another one.'

A red Ford Ka <u>was</u> seen near the bank and <u>was</u> later found in a car park at Heathrow Airport. A reward is <u>being</u> offered by the police for any information about the crime.

Unit 12

The sounds /e/ and /eɪ/

2 [T12.1]

1	sell	sail	sell
2	pen	pain	pain
3	shade	shed	shade
4	tell	tail	tail
5	letter	later	letter
6	paper	pepper	paper
7	well	well	whale
8	test	test	taste
9	wet	wait	wet
10	gate	get	gate

4
1 a   2 b   3 a   4 b   5 b   6 a

5 [T12.5]
/e/: let, head, says, said, health, very, anywhere, again*, jealous
/eɪ/: cake, great, danger, steak, weight, again*, train, explains

*again can be pronounced either with /e/ or /eɪ/.

Words with silent letters

1 [T12.6]

castle	comb	wrist
daughter	might	fruit
opera	cupboard	bought
listen	foreigner	friend
designer	handsome	suit
whale	lamb	white
could	night	wrong
scissors	cheque	two
answer	champagne	yoghurt

Linking in phrasal verbs

1 [T12.7]
1 Please come in, I was waiting for you.
2 I'm afraid I threw it away yesterday.
3 I'll take out the bottles when I pick up the children.
4 I looked it up but it isn't in the dictionary.
5 Where are your gloves? Put them on before you go out.

2 [T12.9]
1 Put them_on!
2 Take them_off!
3 Pick them_up!
4 Turn_it_off!
5 Switch_it_on!
6 Fill_it_in!
7 Work_it_out!
8 Put_it down!
9 Look_it_up!

4 [T12.10]
1 Throw out the rubbish!
   I've already thrown it out.
2 Pick up your toys!
   I've already picked them up.
3 Will you take back those shoes?
   I've already taken them back.
4 Could you take off your shoes?
   I've already taken them off.

Unit 13

The sound /h/

1 [T13.1]

hotel	homeless
who	hospital
half	heaven
happy	hurts

Note
In the words *honest* and *hours* the letter *h* is silent.

In standard English, the words *where, what, why, when, which* are pronounced with an initial /w/ sound. In some accents – Scottish for example – they are pronounced with an initial /hw/ sound.

3 [T13.2]
1 His house is at the top of the hill. ✓
2 /x/ello Peter! /x/ow are you?
3 It's very / /ot in / /ere.
4 /ʃ/e's in hospital.
5 I've got an / /orrible headache.
6 I / /ad a hamburger for lunch.
7 My hotel's near the school. ✓
8 My / /usband's /h/a doctor.
9 How did you get home? ✓

Note
In 5, 'an' is wrong. We say: *a horrible …*

4 [T13.3]
1 Have I helped?
2 I hate eating hamburgers!
3 Has Abigail hoovered in here?
4 Alan Harbord adores his Aunt Hannah.
5 Old Harriet Elston had a heart attack.
6 Anna hurriedly asked Helmut about his English homework./ Helmut hurriedly asked Anna about his English homework.

Counting syllables

1
businessmen (3)
chocolate (2)
comfortable (3)
conference (2)
delicious (3)
dictionary (3)
different (2)
documentary (4)
fashionable (3)
favourite (2)
interested (3)
marriage (2)
medicine (2)
millionaire (3)
miserable (3)
restaurant (2)
several (2)
temperature (3)

3
1 This chocolate is delicious! ✗
2 Are you interested in marriage? ✓
3 Here's some medicine for your temperature. ✗
4 It's a fashionable restaurant. ✗
5 He's a miserable millionaire. ✓
6 It's a different sort of dictionary. ✗
7 Several businessmen were there. ✗
8 It was a documentary about a sales conference. ✓
9 She felt comfortable in her favourite chair. ✗

Four-syllable words

2 `T13.7`

● ● ● ●
biography
communicate
efficiently
extravagant
impossible

● ● ● ●
advertising
concentrating
decorator
everybody
fortunately
graduated
supermarket

● ● ● ●
absolutely
conversation
disappointing
education
independence
optimistic

Corrective stress

1 `T13.9`

1
No, it's Mr P Blake, 46 Shakespeare Road, London SW3.

2
No, it's Mr P Blake, 46 Shakespeare Road, London SW3.

3
No, it's Mr P Blake, 46 Shakespeare Road, London SW3.

4
No, it's Mr P Blake, 46 Shakespeare Road, London SW3.

5
No, it's Mr P Blake, 46 Shakespeare Road, London SW3.

6
No, it's Mr P Blake, 46 Shakespeare Road, London SW3.

3 Your question should start *Hello. Is that ...* followed by the same telephone number, but with **one different** number where Brian has the stress.

Unit 14

The sounds /ɒ/, /ɔ:/, and /əʊ/

1 `T14.2`

1	/ɒ/	clock	6	/əʊ/	joke
2	/ɔ:/	sport	7	/ɒ/	box
3	/əʊ/	boat	8	/əʊ/	shown
4	/ɔ:/	saw	9	/ɔ:/	born
5	/ɒ/	got	10	/əʊ/	coat

4 `T14.3`

/ɒ/: quarrel, wrong, novel, want, gone
/ɔ:/: walk, thought, water, all, door
/əʊ/: ago, moment, won't, only, phone, although

Words often confused because of their pronunciation

2
1	chief	4	soup	7	recipe
2	kitchen	5	desert	8	diary
3	work	6	quiet		

Hearing *'d* (*had* or *would*)

1 2 a 3 a 4 b 5 a 6 b 7 a

Sound symbol page

1 Tom likes writing poetry.
2 Jane's got a friendly brown pet cat.
3 Sue was fast asleep when the burglars came.
4 Joe bought a bottle of Hungarian wine last night.
5 Liz wants to be rich and famous one day.
6 Paul's a wealthy young tourist.
7 Tom and Liz are good at Spanish.
8 Joe works in a noisy garage.